I LOVE JESUS, BUT I NEED THERAPY

Nicole N. Nelson

Thank You
for your support

- N

I LOVE JESUS, BUT I NEED THERAPY

by Nicole N. Nelson

Published by One Faith Publishing

Richmond, VA

onefaithpublishings@gmail.com

This book or parts thereof may not be reproduced in any form, stored in a retrieval system, or transmitted in any forms by any means -electronic, mechanical, photocopy, recording, or otherwise-written without written permission of the publisher or author, Nicole N. Nelson, except as provided by United States of America copyright law.

Unless otherwise, note that all Scriptural quotations are from the King James Version (KJV) used by permission of the public domain.

DEDICATED
TO MY THREE HEARTBEATS

TABLE OF CONTENTS

FOREWORD

I LOVE JESUS, BUT I NEED THERAPY

In an age when the discussion of Mental Illness is not fully understood and or articulated, Nicole Nelson, with a level of life changing transparency, gives us a glimpse of her journey.

Her subsequent identification of the onset of mental illness, her challenges and her victories allow her to give insight to others in order to assure them that they are not alone.

As she weaves the uniqueness of her self-written poems throughout various chapters, Nicole lets us realize her actual times of vulnerability as well as the underlying strength and determination that she possesses to "not give up"!

I Love Jesus but I need Therapy, is a very informative book and I recommend it to individuals who desire just a little more understanding of how to interact with those affected by this disease.

Dr. Barbara J. McClain,

Founder Barbara McClain Ministries

San Antonio, TX

DIGGING DEEP

For over a decade, I've always assumed that my first encounter with depression was at the age of 17 until the day I was digging through some of my old poems in my very first poetry journal. This was also the day I came to a sad conclusion that; no, the depression didn't start in my late teens; instead, it had been there all the while, and somehow it was able to hide in my shadow without a name or title.

Many couldn't identify my issue, so they brushed my behavior off as common, or I was simply labeled as an odd or emotional child. I can remember writing my first poem in middle school while I attended a summer camp called Camp Coca Cola. Now, you may be asking, what is the relevance of these details. Well, eventually, you will see how poetry allowed me to bury this demon called "Mental Illness." Through metaphors, prose, stanza, and college-ruled notebooks, I etched my unheard tears in every word.

Wait, before I get all deep on you allow me to share some personal insight. I think it would be good to know my background story and the essence that makes up who I am as a person. I grew up pretty normal. My mother has three children: Nico, Nino, and myself. I am the oldest of seven siblings, which includes my father's children. My mother was pregnant with me at 15 and gave birth at 16. My parents married young, and as the story goes, my parents married twice...I guess that means they really loved each other, huh?

To say the least, my father was a drug dealer and a womanizer, so their marriage was short-lived. My mother raised me to be perfect, and I truly believe her intentions were good. She taught me to love God, appreciate everything He blesses us with, work hard, and have integrity, and always keep a clean house. If it wasn't for my strict upbringing and discipline, I wouldn't be the minister/evangelist that I am today. Although her intentions were good, it applied unnecessary pressure to perform as the oldest, and in some ways, it developed an overachiever perfectionist within me. It was in my adolescent years that I cultivated a people-pleasing spirit, and I also quickly learned a bad habit of suppressing my emotions.

This leads me to the first poem I ever wrote, *No One To Talk To*. I don't know why I chose this title, but obviously, I was going through some deep stuff. Meaning, the kind of things that couldn't be translated into speech, but only with a pencil and paper. It's funny because I remember sending my father a copy of my poem. At the time, my dad was in prison, and I could never fathom the weight of my words at such a tender age. My dad was so bothered by my writings that he called my mom to inquire about what was going on with me.

It's kind of funny because he understood how to read in between my fancy wordplay and really see that I was crying out for help. My mother, of course, just brushed it off and assured my father they were just mere words, and I agreed. Maybe I agreed because I believed the words of my mother or I didn't want to worry my father, either way, I assured him they were just words and not to worry. Unfortunately, this was my first lesson on how to become a pro at suppressing my feelings.

On the following page, you'll find a copy of the poem that got my dad so worked up.

No One To Talk To

No one to talk to

No one to talk to when I'm all alone

No one to talk to even when I'm gone

No one to talk to when the tears are rolling down my face

No one to talk to when I'm feeling the pain of rejection

No one to talk to when I'm having guy problems

No one to talk to when I'm hurting on the inside

and yet dare to show it on the outside.

No one to talk to when I have just been approached by peer pressure.

No one to talk to when I feel like I want to break down and cry.

No one to talk to when I feel that no one just doesn't understand me

Just no one to talk to.

As I look back over that poem, I believe that I was going through depression, yet, I was trying to find a way to get a grip on things. Depressed children are overlooked because some people don't like to believe that kids go through depression too. Today, I could care less of trying to attempt to dispel the ignorance of those that buy into this theory. Instead, I can only allow the writings to speak for itself.

WHERE IT ALL BEGAN

spent years trying to communicate through the spoken words, "I love Jesus, but I need therapy." During the summer months, I searched as I tried to find myself through my writings. Looking back, I wish my mom would have given my dad more props to see something that maybe her eyes were dismissing as an emotional child. Perhaps a second look would have prevented the toxic relationship I had with mental illness, or maybe I would have embraced the power of my words and emotions. Those thoughts often plagued my mind, but when it's all said and done, I have to take rest in the fact that Romans 8:28 rings true, *"And we know that all things work together for good to them that love God, to them who are the called according to His purpose."*

So, let's dive into when I officially identified that something wasn't quite right with me and the abnormal things I was experiencing. I recall my senior year of high school because I went through some rough moments. It seems like depression and I became the best of friends because I began to distance myself from my real friends and family. I was so depressed that I would purposely sit at a table by myself in the senior cafeteria to avoid reacting and going off on people. So, I thought it would be best for everyone if I just sat by myself.

Well, wouldn't you know, the pesky three is what I called them at the time Cherrell Evans, Brian Herndon, and Ashley Mitchell would always come to my table and try to cheer me up. Daily they would try to get me out of this funk of depression. I remember going off on Cherrell so she could leave me alone and just let me sit in peace. I asked, why do you guys insist on bothering me every day? I just want to be left alone. Eventually, my rudeness worked, and they stopped visiting my table. I wish my 17-year-old self knew now what I didn't know back then.

This Nicole was someone who saw beyond my rude behaviors and attempted to brush them off. This was love in action! I am extremely grateful for the pesky three because they never gave up on me, and daily they invaded my space with hugs. Little did they know that those hugs kept me going, literally. I would like to give a big shoutout to their parents, who raised them to be kind and compassionate at a time when individuals are self-absorbed and selfish!

So, I know you're thinking. girl, you were just going through typical teenage mood swings, but wait, there is more. The sitting alone in the cafeteria was just one little thing I did, among many other things. I remember lashing out at my counselor while in his office. You see, the conversation was centered around the recent decline in my grades, and his concern was if I would graduate. I literally told this white man that he didn't know what it was like to spend a day in my shoes, and graduating was the least of my concerns.

See, at that time, I was living with my aunt Shari because my mom had been tripping and kicked me out of the house. I was living out this little suitcase in which I only had a few outfits and a hot three to four pairs of underwear that I hand-washed before school.

I was sinking into a mental dark hole. Yes, I went to school, but I was very depressed. I stopped doing my schoolwork and just did the bare minimum. Daily, I was shrinking, and most people didn't notice until my grades started to slip, which leads me to a bigger episode.

It was a regular day in my English class, and my teacher was this older white man with glasses and a long beard. I recall his lectures being very boring, and I often questioned the purpose of attending his class, or maybe it was just the depression talking. Well, I don't remember what happened exactly, but I excused myself from his class and went to the restroom.

The restroom was literally the next room over from my class, so I went intending to give myself a pep talk, but I broke down instead. My little body slid onto that nasty restroom floor that probably had never seen a day of pine sol, bleach, or any good ole elbow grease a day in its life. That day I cried some ugly tears, it felt like I had been in that restroom a lifetime, and apparently, I was gone so long that the teacher sent my friend to check on me.

Now, pause because what you are about to read, I must give a disclaimer because although I want to speak my truth candidly, I also want to protect those whose names I mention.

We were kids at the time, and although we may have meant well, no one educated us on depression, the signs of it, or how to deal with empathy. Okay, now conclude. So, my friend enters the bathroom and finds my pitiful self on the floor, crying my eyes out. I mean, I'm crying like I just lost my momma. As my friend reached for me, she said, "Girl, get up off this dirty floor! Ain't nothing wrong with you; you will be alright." Little did she know that scene in the bathroom was a desperate cry for help. It was also my depression showing up in other ways. Let's just say, this may have been my 1st panic or anxiety attack, but I didn't learn the definition of depression until my late 20's.

After I graduated high school, I moved with my grandmother. My mother and I didn't see eye to eye during this time, and I had nowhere else to go. God bless a granny that asks no questions and only does what good grannies do; protect and help their babies. I showed up to my granny house with once again that same pitiful Mary Kate and Ashley suitcase and the few clothes my mom allowed me to grab.

You see, before showing up at my granny's crib, I felt unwelcomed at my aunt's house, but I definitely couldn't go back to my momma's place. Shoot, even my stylist told me that day that I couldn't stay with her, and I needed to go back from where I came from. So, my stubborn 18-year-old self, decided that instead of going back to my aunt's home who loved me dearly, I allowed pride to convince me to sleep in the park. Crazy, I know, right.

Whew, chile, pray for your children; this is why the blood is necessary. Well, my best friend Erica, who had way more sense than me, begged me not to sleep in the park, but go to my granny's house instead. Now, you can understand why I am so grateful for the fact that my grandmother and I never shared words that night, but her eyes reassured me that everything would be alright. Granny, if you are reading this chapter, that was the wisdom of the Lord.

For seven years, I lived with my grandmother, and while I was there, I went through some of the darkest depression in my life!! I often wondered why my granny didn't take notice of the fact that I slept a lot, displayed no interest in eating at times, and lacked a social life. During those seven years, I wrote a lot of dark poetry. One poem I wrote was "Suicidal Thoughts," I wrote this poem while working at Walgreens after experiencing a panic attack in the bathroom.

SUICIDAL THOUGHTS

As my body slid down the wall of Walgreens bathroom stall

Tears rolled down my eyes because I just felt like giving up.

Giving up on my dreams, family, this damn job, and the idea that I can do all things through Christ who strengthens me.

You see, my body has grown accustomed to feeling this way.

A sense of no hope and shit, why should I cope with the ignorant people in my life anyway?

A friend once told me that if my thoughts were suicidal, then not to text her.

Cause if I was going to do it, I would have done it already anyway.

Now, I don't know about you, but maybe I just didn't sound convincing enough.

Maybe she didn't know this idea had crossed my mind way too many times before two much.

So now I sit with a bottle of Advil in my hand. Thinking if I should rewind, fast forward, then press play.

I can erase these suicidal thoughts which have come across my mind today.

And all the bad things that have ever happened to me.

Starting with my father going to prison at 10, being taken advantage of way too many times to count, and let's not forget, almost getting raped!

Though at the end of the day, it saddens me that no one will hasten, stop, and take notice of my present status today.

Cause like yah said the average person wouldn't write a poem or talk about suicide.

They would just do it anyway.

Suicidal thoughts...

Wow, it's crazy because I haven't been back to that Walgreens since the day it happened. However, I vividly remember being stressed about work and my life and hiding in the bathroom while having an anxiety attack on the bathroom floor for what felt like forever. I also vividly remember calling my friend after work to ask how many pills I would need to swallow in order to take my life. You see, she was a nurse, so I knew of course if anyone knew, she would. She jokingly asked why I wanted to know. I tried to take my life that day after work, but I didn't have the courage to take all those pills; instead, I left the house and roamed the streets until I ended up behind a dumpster on Olive.

Unexpectedly, I found a joint on the ground that I attempted to light and smoke. To this day, I don't know if that joint was laced with crack or not, but I am telling you, God protects babies and fools because I never got that stupid thing to light. I even took it upon myself to curse God because I couldn't get high. So, I thought that I must truly be a failure, I can't take my life because I'm a punk and I can't even get high.

I don't quite remember how many suicide attempts I had in my teenage years, but my relationship with depression, suicide, panic attacks, and anxiety was just getting started, which leads me to my first interactions with social anxiety. My Psych doctor taught me that fancy term, but to black folks, I was just weird, odd, but eccentric was the word I chose to adopt. I've always liked that word better than weird. To this day, the word "weird" is like a fighting word for me. You would think someone called me a (b##ch) the way that word gets me all worked up, I guess, because it was a word that was used to belittle and bully me in middle and high school.

I have been socially awkward for as long as I can remember. I have also dealt with social anxiety for what seems like a lifetime, but I don't believe I was always like this. However, I do believe at one time I was a free and quirky child growing up, but even then, my father would often call me weird. The word didn't faze me back then because I didn't know the weight a word carries.

Now, remember how I told you about how I was raised. Well, my mom was old school and strict! Like many mothers that grew up in her era, children were to be seen and not heard. So, this next story has nothing to do with social anxiety. I remember one time my mom flipped out when she caught me writing on the side of our apartment building. The lady that owned the building told her I drew a whole little mural, as I was the modern-day hood, Picasso. I discovered that you could rub rocks on the brick to write because the rocks produced white chalk. So, consider yourself lucky for the kids that grew up with sidewalk chalk. It probably was the byproduct of kids that got their butt whopped for trying to be creative like me. To make a long story short, my mother made me rub off the entire mural with some newspaper. At that time, I'd rather for her to just whoop me because my little hands and arms resented that mural for how long it took to clean it off.

Okay, so back to discussing how social anxiety came about. Sorry, I am longwinded, as you can see, but if you must read a book about mental health, at least let it be interesting, right? So, my mother was strict, and she always did things that I hated! We would be at church or some kind of important event, and she would always scold me for not interacting with people. She would say that she didn't understand why I acted that way. I guess, in a sense, it embarrassed my mother to have people question your child's awkwardness.

It wasn't that I was rude; I just didn't care to engage in conversation with a large crowd. It always made me anxious, and it made me feel like I would literally pass out, and I was always ready to leave. My mother loved to fellowship after church and talk with the ladies, and she loved to brag on me and show me off. Lil Erica and the little minister is what they called me, or they often asked, "So, are you going to be a minister like your mother?" I would just shove my shoulders and say, "I don't know, I guess." I would say anything to make them stop engaging me in conversations.

Now, if you think that was bad, I also remember a time when my mother recognized my talent for poetry. Whenever my mother had company over, she would yell for me to come upstairs. I already knew this was a code to do a poem for her friend because she just spent hours bragging about me. This annoyed me because reciting a poem in front of her company was like getting your tooth pulled. Still, I always obliged to my mother's request and said one of her favorite poems. I could see a gleam of excitement in her eyes as her guest complimented me on my literary skills. I often told myself those little moments of my mother's acceptance caused me to continue putting myself through the awkwardness of the encounters I hated. My mother was my biggest hero, and I always sought to make her proud of me in everything I did.

2 LEFT FEET

ike depression, social anxiety made life very hard for me. When I became an adult, my childhood friends loved to kick it, and by that, I mean clubs and bars. They were always talking me into going out, despite the fact that those places were never my choice of scene, but I was obliged to their request. Here it goes, that people-pleasing thing showing up again. At every bar and club, I always stood out like a sore thumb.For starters, PK kid that's short for "preachers' kid," I can't assume that everyone who's reading this book knows church slang.

On top of that, I hated large crowds, but I loved my childhood friends Kelly, B., and Chris, my three amigos. We had known each other since forever. I met Chris in the 4th grade and B. and Kelly in the 6th grade, and they have always accepted my awkwardness and social anxiety. My clique always had my back, and to them, my eclectic ways made me cool and unique, and not weird like the rest of society portrayed me to be. Still, I hated those dang clubs. I hated how I clung to the nearest corner in the room. I hated how outsiders always picked up on the fact that I didn't say much and often turned down drinks, or the opportunity to dance, besides, dancing made me feel anxious. Who deemed public dancing as fun anyway? It always gave me the worst anxiety, and I could only do it when I was super drunk, and by the way, my friends loved it when I was a Lil tipsy because I would loosen up as they say.

Sadly, anxiety trickled over into my relationships because I hated to show any type of public affection. One time my boyfriend yelled at me about how I wasn't affectionate enough, and he always got pissed about how I could easily explain my emotions through poetry, but never in person. Little did he know that I was trying to navigate through life and deal with anxiety; the best way I knew how. So, what deviated us from holding hands while walking was hyperhidrosis, which is nothing but a fancy word for "I sweat a lot," and when I'm nervous, my hands become clammy. Since we're on the topic of anxiety, let me tell you about a story that is centered around my social anxiety.

There once was this guy named "Pretty Reece, " which is what we called him. He was a teddy bear kind of guy with a nice smile and could dress his butt off. Well, Pretty Reece had a crush on me and asked me to homecoming, and why did my silly self turn him down? And my cousin Mimi was not happy to hear that, so she insisted that I go with him to the homecoming dance. Eventually, I told Mimi that I declined his offer, and not because I didn't like him. Yes, he was very attractive, but I declined because I couldn't dance. So, my cousin made it her mission to teach me how to dance before homecoming night. I walked to Pretty Reece's house, and I told him the real reason why I declined his request, and he just laughed. He said that he didn't care if I could not dance; he just wanted to take me to homecoming. On the night of the dance, my nerves were shot, and I didn't want to dance the entire night, and my social anxiety was kicking in at a level 20!

Eventually, I felt horrible for the poor guy, so my cousin convinced me to at least do one slow song with him, and I did, even though I kept stepping on his feet the entire time, and it felt like I was going to pass out. I apologized to him and suggested that he should have taken someone else because I was too awkward. I'm not sure ifPretty Reece had any fun or enjoyed himself, but one thing is for certain, he was the perfect gentleman. I eventually realized that I would never be comfortable in social settings. Therefore, I spent the bulk of my teenage years and 20's avoiding kickbacks, clubs, parties, and anything with large groups of people; the only exception was if my three amigos were going or if it was a smaller party.

I mentioned briefly about my run-ins with suicide, so in the next chapter, I will go even deeper into how bad the enemy wanted to take my life. I have heard a lot of people say, those who operate strongly in the prophetic also deal with a lot of mental issues. If you have ever watched the cartoon Dragon Ball Z as a child, let's just say I must be the Goku in the prophetic office. I mean, God must have a crazy call on my life because the enemy became creative and crafty with different ways to take my life. I guess he feared the fact that I would write this book and tell the "naked" truth, a truth that would help, heal, set free, and deliver many.

DELAYED,
BUT NOT DENIED

started college late in life, 23-years-old to be exact. I always wanted to attend college; I even got accepted into Columbia College of Performing Arts, twice. Yes, you heard that right, twice! My reason for not going to college sooner was because my mother refused to help me get into school. I mean, she clowned me the time I tried to register for school and applied for financial aid at Forest Park

College. My mother has always been secretive or a "private person" as she would like to tell it, so when the school wanted to get inside her financial business in order for me to get school aid, she definitely didn't like that.

Long story short, that day ended abruptly at Forest Park Community College. I never was able to register for school, which meant, I spent the next few years trying to get financial help, finally, being able to attend at 23 yrs. old when the state deemed me independent. Which leads me to the one time the enemy tried to take me out before a speaking engagement I had at a church. It was on a Saturday when my roommate and I got into it. I can't even recall what the argument was about, but it was something she said that triggered me in the worse kind of way, and the next thing I knew, just a few hours before my event, I was locked in the 2nd bathroom with a butcher knife to my throat.

Looking back, it seemed to happen so fast. In fact, I don't even remember walking downstairs to the 2nd bathroom in our dorm, nor do I remember where I even got the knife from. However, I do remember talking tc these voices in my head for over an hour, telling them to "shut up" and "No, I won't take my life, just be quiet!"

At that moment, Satan had plans to take me out before I got a chance to speak with the youth. Well, thank God that I had enough sense to call someone who could get a prayer through. Yes, I called my spiritual mother in the gospel, Elder Crystal Coleman, and she talked to me for what felt like a lifetime on that phone. She talked me down and asked me what my location was. I remember just screaming and crying when I called her, I was also talking to myself, and even I couldn't articulate what was going on with me. I just knew I needed prayer immediately. She heard my distress and started calling out my name and asking what was wrong; I couldn't respond, so she began to pray a powerful prayer, decreeing and declaring that I would live and not die.

I can't imagine what went through her mind on the day I called her. As she prayed, the voices in my head stopped, and I was able to put the knife down by throwing it across the bathroom floor. Oh, I forgot to mention that during the mist of this episode, several girls on the other side of the door tried to talk me out of the bathroom stall. I don't know if they actually knew that I was suicidal. I'm telling you there's power in pleading the blood of Jesus; the blood still works.

After I gathered myself, I took a shower and got dressed for my speaking engagement. Hours later, the host of the event asked all the speakers about a time when they really had to trust God, and how He came through. Originally, I was going to speak a cookie cut story to a room of 15-20-year old's, but as the Lord would have it, He told me to talk about how I just tried to take my life 3 hours before the engagement. That moment of raw transparency blessed so many teens; in fact, numerous youths came up and told me their stories about how they had contemplated suicide, and they thanked me for my bravery. God is so awesome with how He uses our trauma and issues to help another if we just choose to be obedient.

Sometimes it saddens me with the number of times I tried to kill myself. Like, I often wondered how I could be this great intercessor and mightily in the prophetic, but every quarter of my life, I'm trying to kill myself. I hope this makes sense, y'all. You know how scripture records, *"For his ways are higher than our ways, and thoughts are not like our thoughts in Isaiah 55:8-9."*

Well, I literally saw this scripture in action the day Jesus told me to tell my current boss that I struggled with mental illness. For the past 11 years, I have worked in Education as a teacher. I have always loved kids but never desired any of my own. I have worked in the public, private, and now the Montessori (Charter) sector, and with all those years of teaching, you would think my spelling and grammar would be better. Seriously, my grammar sucks; this is why I had to hire an editor for this book! Back to my point, at this time, my boss was Dr. Evans, and she was a dope black woman. One of the sweetest bosses I ever worked for, including Inga Gibbs who was the principal of City Garden Montessori

School, where I was an assistant guide in the Primary department working with the littles.

One day the Holy Spirit told me to tell my boss that I needed to talk with her. In this meeting, He instructed me to tell her about my issues with suicide, depression, and anxiety. I was telling this lady all my little personal business. At the time, I didn't quite understand why, but a few weeks later, it all made sense. One day my God-sister was in town for her son's graduation, and for some odd reason, I was highly stressed, and to top it off, I had been triggered. I vividly remember it like yesterday because I was driving Steven's raggedy white "raper van," and I had on all white with my beautiful headwrap to match. Here's why we called the van that name; it was ugly, old because it looked like one of those vans that abduct young girls.

Okay, let's continue; after talking to my sister on the phone, I went inside the house, and instantly all these feelings of depression hit and started to plague my mind. I went from happy to depressed, and from depressed to having an anxiety attack. Everything escalated so quickly, and the next thing I know, I'm literally talking to myself, but this time was even worse than the episode in college; meaning, the voices were stronger, and I was speaking directly to them like we were having a conversation.

At this point, I had totally lost my mind, and with no other options available, I called my best friend Kelly. In the best way possible, I tried to describe what was going on, but apparently, I was so far gone into the conversation that she couldn't understand a word I said. With no avail, I called my homegirl Malerie, and the same thing happened, so I hung up the phone.

Then I heard the Holy Spirit speak, "Call Dr. Evans." Now, I'm really losing it, but apparently, I wasn't that far gone because I had enough sense to question God's request. The Holy Spirit assured me that Dr. Evans could get to me much fast before I tried to kill myself.

To help paint the picture for you, I was sitting on my bed with a knife to my throat and a gallon of bleach. Who knows what I planned to do with that bleach, but I kept brushing the knife against my throat while I was crying and talking to myself. Once I dialed my boss's number, she was able to calm me down long enough to get my address and a few details about the situation. She assured me that she was on her way. Next thing I knew, someone was banging at my door, and I was found on the floor with the knife still in my hand, shaking horribly and talking to myself. Now, at this time, I was completely gone, and all I can remember saying was, "I did good. I did good, right?" I was referring to me calling for help, a statement I spoke at least 20 times in 1 hour while shaking.

My boss held me as she took the knife from my hands, and I just cried and cried out that my life was worthless. After I calmed down, she asked if there was anyone we could call. I told her yes, she could call my God-sister, and that's when the story got worse. Now, most people would say, why would you say that, Nicole? Just wait, you will see.

Whenever my sister shows up on the scene, she snaps at me and tells me that she doesn't understand why I'm pulling this stunt and what this is all about. Now pause, I need you to understand the seriousness of this moment. Once again, for the 50th time, I tried to take my life. My sister, instead of being sympathetic, accuses me of pulling a stunt. This is the same person who I loved, just like my blood sister. This is the same person I've known for well over eight years, and we were like two peas in a pod. Whenever you saw one, you always saw the other. You could call us Gina and Pam off the Martin show, she was my legit rider, or at least I thought.

After a few choices of words were exchanged, she says, "I can't do this!" and walks out of the house, leaving me with my boss. Now, both of us were confused about the situation that had just taken place, and it left me even more traumatized, and I broke!

That night my boss begged me to go to the emergency room or stay with her for the night, and I declined both offers. The reason being, for one, I knew what the hospitals do to folks who try to take their lives; so, there was no way I was agreeing to that one. I also didn't want to feel like a charity case, so I didn't go to my boss's house either. Rather it was pride or stupidity; God still protects babies and fools. So, she agreed to allow me to stay at my apartment, only under her conditions, I answer her calls, and she could remove every cleaning product, knife, and blade out my house.

Guys, I was unable to cut butter, bread, or anything for like a month. This lady literally held my silverware hostage from me. Now, how can you enjoy a good steak with no knife in the house? She meant well, though. The following day at work, she never treated me differently and even assured me it would not have an impact on my job. My boss kept her word, and my coworkers never found out about that night; until a year later, when I decided to share my mental health journey with a coworker.

Looking back on it, I now understand why the Holy Spirit told me to tell my boss that I struggled with depression, anxiety, and suicide. Dr. Evans is the very reason why I had the courage to write this book. Dr. Evans has supported me from day 1 of my journey to being mentally stable. She also told me to just write and worry about the other stuff later. I guess, in a sense, she is like the "work" mom I never wanted (just playing). She always checks up on my well-being and encourages me to take my meds. It's hard to say "No" to this persistent lady. I guess that's why we share the same first name; we're just two relentless individuals in whatever we choose to pursue.

BETTER DAYS

The last suicide story I will share with you is the one that changed my life forever. It is an attempt that I completely thought out, I wrote letters to my family and a will, but this attempt also led me to seek mental help services. So, after the episode in Chapter 4, I spent weeks in my apartment on Michigan Avenue after having anxiety and panic attacks at work. What once was just a little secret that no one knew about was now a secret that was coming to the surface. My mental illness was now showing up on my job, at church, and anywhere else; I assumed I did a great job of hiding it.

One time my mind was so gone, I came to a church service with the intent to end my life. For me, even this was a first because the church has always been a safe place from the enemy. But, not anymore; throughout that entire service, I begged God to take my life because I hated it here. I remember Prophetess Victoria picked it up in the spirit and called me to the altar. She began to pray the prayer of deliverance over me along with the 1st lady. The enemy had such a hold on me that I refused to open my mouth, worship, or do any of the things the woman of God was instructing me to do. I was bitter and angry with God, and I was tired of living and existing.

Eventually, I received a breakthrough at the altar, but I guess that just made Satan madder because he came at me even harder. With everything that was going on in my life, my work ethic began to decline drastically, and my co-workers complained to the boss about my performance. They even addressed their concerns about my recent behavior. Operating out of anxiety and fear losing my job, I put in my two months' notice. That was probably one of the dumbest and most impulsive decisions I have ever made, and I have made many! This one decision caused a ripple effect on my life for nine months.

Once I left City Garden, I thought that I was living on top of the world. I had just registered and received my 501(3)c status for my non-profit. I moved into my dream loft downtown with two bedrooms and two full baths with a beautiful open concept and the most amazing hardwood floors. I also stayed on the 13th floor with a view that wrapped around the entire apartment. Life was sweet, and I was marching to the beat of my own drum. You couldn't tell me anything at that time. I had done everything they said I wouldn't do, and my faith allowed me to get my dream place. I told everyone the testimony about how God blessed me with my loft, and I stepped out on faith to start my business.

Looking back on it, was it really faith, or just another one of my impulsive moves where God allowed grace to abide? The loft was a faith move, and God did move mightily;however, I left my job prematurely and ignored the words of the prophet that I should not quit in December. But I was so stressed out and tired of having panic attacks at work that I literally convinced myself that God gave me the month of December to leave. Here's the thing about anxiety; it will have you doing and believing all types of crazy things.

So here comes February, it comes, and everything hits the ceiling in the perfect little bubble I created for myself. The government came after me and took my entire $2,000 tax return that I owed for student loans, and I didn't even know that they could do that! See, all those days I spent depressed at the apartment on Michigan Avenue and not opening my mail came back to haunt me. Had I opened my mail; I would have known they sent a final notice warning me they could potentially take my refund. Also, if I had been more proactive in my depression, I could have avoided it all by opening up my mouth and talking to someone before I filed my taxes. Pride and anxiety never make a great combination. Not a day goes back that I don't replay that scene out a thousand times in my head.

Everything quickly spiraled out of control as I got behind on my rent, and the money I was making from Airbnb just wasn't cutting it. A friend of mine helped me raise over $300 towards my rent, but that still wasn't enough. The rent for that fancy loft was $1,000, which would not have been a problem if I didn't quit my job. So again, my old friend, depression, came to visit me, and this time he came with a vengeance. I spent days in my loft, depressed, sad, and suicidal. I wouldn't eat, shower, or socialize. My friend, Stazhia, tried to help me during this time, but I was too far gone. One night, she sat with me for hours while I contemplated suicide while she took down her braids because she refused to take my no for an answer.

You see, we need friends like her, friends that will show up to your house unannounced and intrude on your pity party.

Stazhia was my saving grace at the time, and to this day, I love her for that.

Still, it only got worse, and within a few days of coming up for air and having some sense of normalcy, I just got tired of literally smelling myself because I hadn't showered for 24 hrs., so I had to force myself to take a shower. I cried so long and hard in that shower, but my wallowing wasn't enough, so I began to research ways to kill myself. If someone hacked my phone and searched my history, I'm pretty sure they would have thought that something was sick and wrong with me. I looked up ways to strangle myself, jump from buildings, and the chances of survival. I became so engulfed with suicide that it was sickening. I began to prepare my mind, so I started placing my affairs in order. I wrote like a total of 6 letters to my childhood friends and a few family members.

When you have been contemplating suicide for a long time, and you start to write those letters, you realize who you love the most and who truly cares. I wrote a letter to Stazhia, Kelly, Bre, Erica, Gina, and I believe my mom. I don't even think I wrote one to my siblings. I only took the time to write to the people who dared to take notice of the signs of my mental illness, and only those people deserved a letter.

I eventually settled with jumping out of the window, a window that was located by my couch in the living room. The chances of me dying were good, and someone would find the body on the street. I also left my door open with the letters placed where they could be easily found. As I sat on the ledge of that building for what felt like hours, I cried because I badly wanted to jump, but couldn't bring myself to do it because I didn't want to go to hell. I mean, I've spent years of my life ministering to people about the gospel, only to go out like that.

The Bible says that if you take your life, you will surely go to hell or something like that. It's crazy because the only saving grace at that moment that brought me back to my right mind was a picture of my God-sister. God used the love I had for her and the fact that she had just lost her mom a few weeks prior, and that's what caused me not to jump. I didn't want her to bury her mom and me in the same month because that would be cold.

I LOVE JESUS,
BUT I NEED THERAPY

y childhood friend, Erica, who is also the mother of my beautiful God-son Legacy. At the time, she had never witnessed any of my episodes, and she was my oldest friend of 20 years. Well, one day, that all change; while I was having a panic attack, I called Erica, who conveniently lived in the same building as my loft, and only two floors beneath me. I couldn't articulate what I was actually going through, but I asked her to come and sit with me, and she did, but she also cried an ugly cry. You know the cry when someone loses a person dear to them. She cried as she witnessed all my triggers and mannerisms in one full sitting. I never felt so naked, hopeless, and exposed. Yes, I had a serious problem, and I needed help, so Erica and Kelly, along with my church member Tutu pleaded with me that I couldn't keep doing this to myself, and eventually, the suicide attempts would be successful, but they loved me too much for that! Tutu told me about BJC Behavioral Health, who helps people that struggle with mental illness like me, and I promised her I would go.

I don't know if it was me writing those letters to my loved ones or losing my dream loft, but I realized my problems were now beyond my unhealthy coping mechanisms. I went to BJC, not knowing what to expect and got some help. Since then, I have been taking meds, seeing a therapist, and psychiatrist. You see, I love me, some Jesus, but I also needed therapy. They diagnosed me with PTSD, severe depression, and social anxiety. I wasn't sold on taking meds right away, but I decided to put myself on them with the help of my doctor's advice.

In today's society, despite all the progressive thinking, access to information, and social rebels, Mental Health is still very much a taboo, especially in the black community.

You would think being diagnosed, that my life would become a lot easier for me, but I was just getting started on my mental health journey. In this section, I will dive into all the uphill battles I have experienced in advocating for myself, my disability, and the long-term effects it has had in my family.

Every family has that one cousin or family member that we all have labeled "touched" or just a Lil crazy. We jokingly introduce them this way to others outside the family to provide this bootleg disclaimer on why they are the way they are. Most black folks don't believe in therapy, and we definitely disagree with telling all our business to some "white" shrink in most cases. Black people have this stigmatism when it comes to mental illness. We have convinced ourselves that our "blackness" and strength have made us exempt, and for the rare few, it does impact that they are the exception to the rule because they just weren't strong enough not to break.

In my family, I have several aunts on my father and mother's side that deal with mental illness. One of my favorite aunts has tackled mental illness for the last seven years, and it forever changed her life when she was in high school. I even have a cousin whom I believe may or may have a personality disorder. Regardless black folks don't allow you to claim you're depressed, and in some ways, they disregard the real impact it has on your life. If you say you struggle with mental illness, most automatically assume bipolar or schizophrenia disorder because they are the only two mental illnesses we have legitimized in our communities as real mental disorders. And in the church, it seems we have taken our consideration of mental health to the extreme. See, the black church doesn't do mental illness either. We prescribe to the belief that Jesus heals all things and which he does! We also believe that you can just simply pray or exorcise those demons away through deliverance ministry.

Well, I consider myself to be a devout Christian saved, baptized, and filled with the Holy Ghost with the evidence of speaking in tongues, but I have struggled with mental illness for over a decade! Yes, I have done all the altar calls and even begged God to take this thing away from me, but I was only left with anger from trying to figure out why God allowed this to be so.

Yes, I believe prayer is very effective, paired with therapy, and even medication for some. However, I do NOT prescribe to the theory that just because I love Jesus, I don't need THERAPY. Jesus has given us doctors, therapists, and even medicine to help in our mental health journey. Some people God may choose to heal automatically, and for others, we should not feel ashamed or ostracized for seeking outside help in our journey. We don't, in return, have less FAITH, and

God doesn't deem us any less mature or seasoned than the next saint.

I don't know why I deviated from the task to give this subject its own attention, but apparently, it needs to be discussed. The church has failed and will continue to fail if the saints keep pushing this perspective that Jesus and therapy cannot be synonymous with one another.The same Jesus I have been serving the bulk of my life led me to therapy and to take meds. He also encouraged me that my journey with mental illness was not in vain, but to dispel the ignorance within the church and the black community. To pull the wool off the eyes of His people that we have willingly agreed to wear in an attempt to remain comfortable and not discuss those hard topics. I hate to say it, but if my faith was not strong in Jesus, I would have renounced the church because of the ignorant comments that have been made about the denial of my disability.

Oh, and the church is not the only one I have had to advocate my mental health to constantly. I now have family and friends that question the legitimacy of what I struggle with daily. Recently I even had an employer say to me during an interview that, "Well, I can't see your disability." That comment angered me and furthered solidified why the writing of this book is necessary. There are so many people that suffer in silence with mental illness. Just because you can't see a disability doesn't negate the fact that it is very real and impacts our lives daily.

On one occasion, I had to stand up for myself and even hold my ground with my favorite cousin. You see, I had just left the barbershop and got a bad haircut. The cut was fire, but it just didn't fit my face. For anyone that knows my cousin, she is very opinionated and blunt. My cousin, after seeing my hair went on and on about how she hated it and how the barber should have never allowed me to leave his chair like that. She antagonized me so much to the point I began to have an anxiety attack in her kitchen. Next thing I know, my breathing became irregular, and tears began to stream down my face.

My younger cousin, her daughter, came in the kitchen to give her opinion on my haircut as well, and I quickly realized that I was being triggered. She offered to give me some of her medication, but I declined. It's crazy because before all that happened, I remember yelling at my cousin. She was triggering my anxiety, and the next thing I knew, I couldn't breathe. To my dismay, I had left my meds at home. I started panicking and so I immediately began to do the breathing exercises I was taught, and it took me over 30 min to come down from that attack.

I declined my cousin's ride to take me home, so I left her house and decided to take the bus home instead. I felt like my feelings and mental health had been completely disregarded at that moment. To wrap the story up, in light of the recent metro changes, the bus had stopped running by my cousin's house. So, I had to make that dreadful walk back to her house and ask for a ride. When I got back, she fussed at me some more, asking where I had been. She said my cousin, her daughter, had gone off on her for pushing me too hard and being rude to me. She even blamed her for my abrupt departure. My cousin apparently was out driving the streets looking for me along with her boyfriend. No one knew where I had gone. I could have sworn I told them I was leaving, but I have been told that I tend not to talk loud enough or assert myself. To think I never thought my Lil cousin even loved me that much. She usually tends to be rude to me and blunt just like her mother.

Well, instead of biting my tongue, I decided to advocate for myself. I did something that day, which was very hard for me; I spoke up! I told my favorite cousin how her actions were belligerent, rude, offensive, and even ignorant. I told her how sometimes she just doesn't know when to stop. Her actions literally gave me an anxiety attack, and what made it worse was when I said she was triggering me. She said, " Oh, Nicky, stay in the kitchen having an anxiety attack." I told my cousin that day how I wanted to tell her in private and not under these circumstances that I have always dealt with this, and its nothing to joke about. My diagnosis was real, and either she could respect, or I just not deal with her at all. My cousin, who was sensing the seriousness of my situation began to apologize. She told me she would never have made a comment about anxiety if she knew it was something I dealt with. She never wanted to hurt my feelings or be rude to me. I was her favorite Lil cousin; she went on to say, " If I piss you off who will come to visit me, you the only Lil friend I got!"

For the 1st time, I felt like my cousin really saw and heard me at that moment. I know she loves me hence why I call her my favorite cousin. I just refuse to have folks disregard my disability because they don't know what it feels like to walk a day in my shoes. I have literally been fighting for my life with this disability!

It's crazy because even my own old therapist at BJC disrespected me during one of our sessions. We were discussing my childhood trauma and how my dad's words really impacted me. We also talked about my social anxiety. At one point, the therapist goes on to say. "This is one of the weirdest sessions I have ever been in." At that moment, his comment angered me! Not only was he unprofessional but, rude as his remarks referred to my body language, disposition, and words during the session. I mentioned how I had social anxiety and how one on ones was hard for me and that it should already be in his notes. He goes on to say, "That explains your behavior."

At times I was mad because I never stood up for myself, and at that moment, I just awkwardly laughed off his comments. Yet, deep down inside, I felt uncomfortable and like that same awkward kid in high school. Some old habits just never leave you because I still hate the word "weird". Let's just say I eventually found my inner strength and fired that therapist!

"DON'T,
HAVE NO KIDS, NICKY!"

My favorite scripture, 2 Corinthians 3:5, has got me through some of my most challenging moments in life; it is also written on my business cards. 2 Corinthians 3:5 talks about how our sufficiency is not of ourselves, but God! Despite that fact, I know that this chapter is probably one of the hardest chapters that I will write in this book. In this chapter, God has been nudging me to speak my truth, a truth that I have kept buried for years. Some of the stories I have chosen to share have never been told to anyone. There are some stories that Ican't bear to think about without feeling hopeless, guilt, and shame. Through my courage, someone else will feel bold enough to share their truth too.

Okay, enough of the sentimental mess, lets dive into the meat and potatoes! Most of my encounters with sex have been non-consensual. It's hard for me to say that because it leaves a bad taste in my mouth.

My first inappropriate encounter was around the age of 7 years old. I was staying over at my aunt's house in the city. Her older son and I were playing wrestling, I was a tomboy, so I often wrestled with my boy cousins for fun. Well, this day wouldn't be like any other wrestling session; instead, this day took something away from me that I can never get back. While my cousin and I were playing, his hands began to roam my pink shorts. He kept trying to do something with my button, but my aunt was calling for us like it was yesterday. She walked in on me in a very awkward position, fully clothed, but my cousin was doing something he shouldn't be doing.

That day he attempted to molest me, and at the time, I knew in some kind of way that his actions were wrong. I often wondered why my aunt never addressed what she walked in and saw, and I even contemplate as to why it took me to be in my 20's to acknowledge this as the first act of a long history of sexual trauma.

The next act didn't occur until I was about eight years old. I actually blocked this incident out my mind, but the Lord brought it back to my remembrance a few months ago. There was a lady who attended my church, and she had many kids. She and my mom were very close, so close that I was allowed to spend weeks at her house and even an entire summer to attend summer camp with the lady's kids.

Well, this woman had an older son who was years older than me. Up until that point, he was like a God-brother to me, and I would have never imagined him hurting me or doing anything inappropriate.

One night, I stayed the night over their house, now, I don't know what was so special about this night, but he came down to his sister's room where I was sleeping and called me in the dark to come upstairs with him. He told me he had a cool game and he wanted me to play with him. I don't know why I never thought about how odd it was for him to wake me up out of my sleep to play a videogame. However, I agreed because I wanted to play with him. We went upstairs to his room, which was in the attic. A few minutes into the game, he began to touch me, I made a comment about it, but he assured me that it was okay. Eventually, I knew the whole situation was totally wrong, and I d dn't want any parts of it! So, I made an excuse that I was sleepy and wanted to go back downstairs. The truth was, I just wanted to get away from him and his roaming hands, so back, I went downstairs to sleep and try to forget about what just happened, but I woke up to someone touching me or trying to touch me under the covers. Behold! This nasty creep was trying to fondle me while I laid in the same bed right next to his sister. This was the first time that I was molested as a child.

As I got older, my relationship with sex was very odd. My mother never taught me about my body. Shoot, I remember coming on my period and being scared because I thought I was dying, but my mother just laughed and said, " You're just coming on your period." I feel like she never talked about sex with me because, truth be told, she had me at 16. Maybe she was afraid that if I knew too much about sex, I would start having sex, who knows. The only sex talk I got was to wait for marriage, and that was it!

When I was 18, during the time I was living, with my granny, there was a girl who lived three houses down from us. My granny was never too fond of her; in fact, we often got into arguments over this young lady. Looking back on it, maybe my granny could see something in her that I was too blind to see at the time. After getting tired of fighting me on the matter, my granny gave in to the fact that I was convinced of being this girl's friend. That same young lady was a lesbian, and why her sexuality is worth mentioning, you will later see.

Quickly, I found out she had a crush on me, but I just wanted to be her friend, so I thought nothing of it. My understanding of sexuality was very ignorant, and years before, I never knew what oral sex was or let alone what two women did together. One day she came over to my house for some reason. This particular day my granny wasn't at home. I remember her pushing up on me really tough. At one point, her behavior became so aggressive that it scared me. She went to turn the lights off in my bedroom and attempted to take advantage of me. To be a skinny girl that only weighed a hot 110 pounds, she was super strong! I remember her pinning me to my bed and trying to force herself on me. I squirmed, twisted, and turned relentlessly. Eventually, I was able to get away from her.

That day my neighbor sexually assaulted me, and what made it even worse, who would ever believe me? My granny warned me not to deal with the girl next door. She always said it was something about her; unfortunately, I had to find out the hard way.

On my street, there were a lot of older couples and people that had lived in their homes for years. I loved living on Braddock because we were like our own little family. The neighbors would give you sugar and eggs to bake a cake, and they even cut your grass when your lawnmower was broken. One particular gentleman that I was really fond of. This man was my papa's friend who lived on our street. My grandfather had a weird obsession with guns and cleaning them. He always mentioned how he would hurt anyone, whoever hurt me in any kind of way. It used to drive me crazy when he would have his guns out, and my boyfriends would come to the house. It also angered my granny because he was an alcoholic, and the gun could accidentally go off one day. Despite his actions being dangerous and reckless, I like to think in his own little way, that's how my papa showed he cared for me. He would always watch movies with me on Friday nights, and he was drunk and all. Usually, he would talk through the whole film, and I would have to tell him to be quiet, but I always looked forward to those bonding moments with him. My papa's favorite question to ask me was, "Nicky, why you in the house on a Friday night?" "You ain't ugly...why you don't have a boyfriend?". That question drove me crazy.

Men always wanted one thing from me, sex, and that's it. At least that's what my experiences taught me, and my naiveness allowed me to let my guard down for my papa's friend. He always gave me a ride to the store to get things for my granny and the house. My grandparents never imagine the neighborhood friendly old man was a pervert and had waited years to make his move on me. See, he used the fact that I trusted him against me. One day while we were riding in his truck, he asked me why I didn't have a boyfriend. Not thinking much of his question, I brushed it off with some reply that would suffice his questioning. Next thing you know, his creepy lil old hands began rubbing my thigh while in the truck. I felt helpless at that moment and anxious to get out of the car.

I never told anyone what happened in that truck or how my papa's friend made a pass at me. Eventually, I just stopped going across the street, and I also stopped asking him for rides or accepting them. My granny even asked me why I chose to walk instead of allowing my grandfather's friend to take me, and I always gave her some odd answer to cause her not to investigate further. Maybe, she chucked it up to my stubbornness or the fact that I was a moody teen, but eventually, she just quit asking why.

To this day, I wish I had the courage to tell my papa how that man violated me in his truck. I guess a part of me knew my grandfather would be in jail if I told him what his friend tried to do. So, I allowed that to be my excuse for years, and I never told a soul until now. It's very hard for me to accept most of my encounters with sex have been unwanted, and people were touching my body as if it was their God-given right to do so. I often blame myself for these encounters. I figured that maybe I did something to deserve these advances. I also blame my ignorance for placing myself in these situations. I figure maybe if I knew more about sex and predators', people would stop touching me in ways that I never agreed to.

For years my mother would introduce me to her friends and brag about my virginity during her introduction. I mean, she talked about my virginity more than I did before I even understood it's worth. I hated how people teased me for still being a virgin after age 18. My mom said it was a blessing because most girl my age was doing; God knows what. The funny thing was I don't ever think I knew what "what" was except for what movies portray. You see, I was just that ignorant of sex. When my friends would talk about sex, they would always joke about protecting my virgin ears. It seems like everyone wanted to protect my "virginity" as if it was some trophy that they controlled.

Isn't it crazy how society and those around me were obsessed with my virginity while I was trying to be educated on what was so special about it? I often tell people that I stayed a virgin until age 18 because of fear and reverence for my mom. After that, I kept my virginity in tack for myself because, in a way, it had always been a part of my identity. I know it may sound pitiful to you, but my virginity was like the one thing I got right, and people respected me for it. Shoot, it even got me cool points with people. I don't know if it was because they were fascinated that I was still a virgin going into my 20's or that the saw pieces of themselves in me. Women would always tell me; I wish I would have held on like you.

My aunt favorite words were, "Don't have no kids, Nicky" is something she would always tell me. With my whole life being centered around this one word, you can see how, when I lost it, how detrimental it was to me. When I was 20, I was dating this rapper. I never could remember his government name, but I met him at the barbershop. I went into the shop one day while he was getting his haircut, and my stylist tried to play wingman with us. After that, we hit it off, and he became my boyfriend... just like that. Back then, my requirements were simple, be cute, have a car, a job, and treat me nicely—nothing like the standard and requirements I now have. Sorry guys let just say he messed that up for a lot of people.

Well, one day, I went over to his house to Netflix and chill. Now I know what you are thinking, that's the code for sex, but remember I was a virgin and a "pk," so we really were just chilling, at least that's what I thought. It was cold when I visited him. It had to be right before winter because I was wearing my cute half black, grey, and red jacket with the fur on the hood, a white shirt, skinny jeans, and some low top denim J's. We sat in his room, as usual. I sat on the edge of the bed, trying to engage in the show or movie he had on, but my boyfriend kept puffing to the point that it pissed me off. I remember asking him if there was a problem, and he responded that I knew what was up. I think I must have yelled at him and even pointed and my vagina, like what is this, what do you want in frustration. The next thing I know, he tackles me to the bed, and we started to wrestle. At some point, it became serious, and I realized this guy had plans to rape me.

Like I remember the look in his eye; the one that had no regard for my body, the same look countless people had given me before him. A survival instinct must have gone off in my head because I began to fight back hard with everything in me. He continued to pull down my pants while I flighted and squirmed, yelling, please don't do this. Somehow, he managed to get my pants off and threw them across the room. I was now half-naked and cold. This next part may be very graphic for some, but I will never forget the size of his penis. It was large and long. I thought to myself, oh God, that's not going inside of me. He pushed my panties to the side and started trying to force his self-inside of me.

Maybe it was just the grace of God, but somehow, after all that wrestling and blacking out in my mind that I was going to be raped helped me to get away. I ran downstairs to the guest bathroom, locked the door, and examined my delicate flower. My underwear had a puddle of blood in it, and I screamed at the sight of the blood. After that, I went into panic mode as I thought of ways to get out of this guy's house. Thankfully, his manager appeared at the apartment, and he asked "the rapper" why I was acting so weird, but he just brushed it off and said he didn't know. I think he even said at one time that I better not tell anyone he had tried to rape me. After checking my phone for the bus schedule, I jetted for the door and ran as fast as I could. I ran for what felt like blocks, without even knowing where the heck I was going. A bus was going down Delmar, and I flagged the driver down. I hopped on the bus and began to weep, and the bus driver yelled out, "Hey Lil momma, are you okay?"I nodded my head and replied, yes. The first person I called was my Godmother, who I tried in so many ways to tell her that I had been raped and what happened, and I will never forget her words, "Maybe it didn't happen like you thought it did." I thought to myself if she didn't believe me then who would?

Do you want to know something crazy about that night that I never told anyone? I went home and showered and threw away the evidence of my rape. Man, I was so stupid! A buddy of mine asked me if I wanted to go to a poetry show, and I agreed. That night, literally hours after my rape, I poured out my bare soul on the stage, hoping someone would hear my cry for help through my words. Hoping someone would read in between what I was saying and not saying, but no one ever noticed. It took for me to slip up on the phone with a conversation I had with poet lightning. After that, she convinced me to write about it. You see four months prior to that day I had been raped.

For four months, I held that secret and never told a soul. I wrote the poem " It wasn't his choice" and literally, I was in tears as I played out scene by scene of the events that happened to me. Years later, that poem would go on to encourage other women to talk about their assault. Many people in the poetry circuit didn't even know the poem was about me because I wrote it in a third person. I guess I had to remove myself from the situation in order to tell my full truth.

Rape is somewhat comical because in most cases the victim always blames themselves. I went on to live with the event that took place on that day for another ten years of awkward sexual encounters with men. My rape changed me, and if you thought I didn't desire sex before it, well, I really didn't afterward. I lived life by the odd motto touch, but not be touched, go far, but not too far.

This is how I navigated through my 20's in relationships. I convinced myself that I would do four-play, close burning, allow a man to fondle me, and later on, even two encounters with oral sex as long as it wasn't penetration. In a way, this is how I coped with my odd relationship surrounding sex. I was afraid of sex and wanted no parts of it unless I was in control. Sex to me was painful and never consensual at the least because this is what life had taught me.

You want to know something really pitiful; my 1st encounter with oral sex was never consensual. Now I know what you're thinking, really...Nicole, come on now. You just are exaggerating the story to make people feel empathy for you. Hey, I wish that was the case, but it wasn't. I told you I was ignorant in the worse kind of way about sex. As the story would go, I was messing with this biker. I met him at Soul Sessions one night while doing poetry downtown. He was speeding on Washington street and caught a glimpse of me and stopped to exchange numbers. Now "the biker" was way older than me. Shoot, to this day, I can remember the age difference, and it was enough to make him more sexually advanced than me. I must have been 19 at the time because I surely wasn't old enough to drink. Well, one day, we went to his crib to do a Netflix and chill, but he had other things on his mind. Now before you yell at me through the pages that I needed to stay away from Netflix and chill, I was naive, y'all. The kind of naive and stupidness you never want your daughters to have. I am the product of what happens when parents don't discuss sex and religion, and the upbringing goes wrong.

The world and my friends taught me about sex, which was the worst way to find out. As we were laying in his bed, he decided to go under the covers. I remember yelling at him and asking what he was doing under there. He assured me that I would like it and to just chill. The next thing I know, he was trying to pull down my panties, and well, you know the rest; no need to turn this into a Zane book. With all the squirming that I was doing, you would think he would get the hint that I was not into what he assumed I would like, so against my own will he gave me oral. In his mind, it would help loosen me up. The last thing I remember him saying to me was that I tasted like strawberries. I sat in the bed feeling violated, naked, cold because it was certainly a breeze down there and once again as if my voice didn't matter.

By now, you should get it, my relationship with sex has always been a complicated one. I have been raped, molested, sexually assaulted by my ex, and even forced to have oral sex twice. One was by a guy, the other by a woman who shall remain nameless. When I look back on all these events, it angers me, and I feel foolish. My own ex-boyfriend at one point in time has convinced himself he never sexually assaulted me, and his urges just took him over at that moment. However, the shivering on my bathroom floor on Michigan was very real to me, and the shower I took in an attempt to wash away his unsolicited advances on my body. I literally relived the rape that I had at 20 again at 29, once again at the hands of someone I trusted. Sometimes I feel like there is not enough therapy to help my jacked-up relationship with sex.

Some men have called me out in the past, and they don't believe that I don't have sexual urges. When in fact, I am the polar opposite, I do have urges just like anyone else. Shoot, my horny teenage years of 18 to mid-20s spoke to that. But I also had things broken inside of me that I question if, in fact, it can be fixed. I am scared to be touched in that way. I am often triggered by the slightest aggressive action from the opposite sex towards me. I always have in the back of my mind what if he tries to rape me. My solution for a long time was just to avoid sex; besides, most men only saw me as something to conquer and some kind of special badge or notch to put on their belt. If they could bag a 20 something-year-old virgin, they would be the man. Sadly, these men never cared about my emotional state.

As I end this chapter, I want people to know... have the courage to be brave, unlike me. Speak up and assert yourself!No always means no, even if you guys are in the middle of sex itself! Any act that is not consensual on your part in my eyes is an assault on your body. People don't understand that this trauma carries over into other aspects of our lives. It dictates how we interact with our partners, family members, and anyone else.

So, the next time you witness someone being distant or maybe even cold in affection, choose empathy over ignorance, and be wise with your word choice. You might just be entertaining someone who has been sexually violated on numerous occasions. If so, they need your patience and not judgment. They need to feel safe and not manipulated in your arms. Ultimately you have to earn their trust sexually.

MY 10-YEAR REUNION

WITH MY RAPIST

ne of my favorite stories in the Bible is the story of Esther. I don't know if the reader of this book is like me, but I have always loved a good underdog story packed with action. I guess this also explains my obsession with action movies. You know the type where some handsome guy always saves the day or the geek who has no life but finally gets his moment to go down in history. These things usually happen in movies like Transformers, Spider-Man: Far From Home, and of course, any ending of a world movie where the doctor predicts some life-threatening virus or climate change, but no one listens until things begin to hit the ceiling. And by that, I mean humans turning into zombies, and for a reason, there is never a dang anti-virus easily accessible. Like why is the whole film centered around finding or keeping the one virus safe? That always irked me. It's as if Hollywood ran out of ideas and just copied off previous scripts because if the traditional storyline isn't broken well, don't try to fix it.

Lastly, can anyone tell me why Peter couldn't get his life together and just tell MJ how he felt? I mean, dude seriously, write a poem or letter it doesn't have to be that difficult, even for true introverts. Listen, I found myself yelling at him countless times during the entire movie for this very reason.

I'm sorry I guess I just had to get that out, back to why I love the story of Esther so much. For those of you not familiar with this book of the Bible, the original king was kicking it with some of his royal buddies. I mean they were getting drunk and living their best life. The king was feeling himself that day and requested his queen to show off her beauty to his pals. I guess Queen Vashti was like any other real black woman who hates to be bothered by her kids for stupid things or anyone else for that matter because she refused to come before the king. Oh, the boy was so embarrassed that he vanished Vashti and then after feeling lonely, he realizes, "Oh crap, I miss her stubborn butt." His boys encouraged him to find a new bride to keep him company. This is where Esther comes in. She gains the favor of the king and stands out amongst all these women. I mean, picture a modern-day Miss America Pageant, but with a New Testament twist! The women all received spices and props to gain the king's attention, and in the end, Esther was chosen.

Throughout the story, Ester's uncle, who also raised her became the enemy of a guy named Haman. Haman is the kind of guy that just can't stand for anyone else to get the shine other than him. He is also a narcissist. He literally has everything but want more. Haman had it out for Esther's uncle Mordecai and plotted to kill him.

To wrap up this lengthy summary, see, this is why Sunday School is so important, saints. Quit oversleeping and hitting the snooze button because now I have to give you the bootleg summaries for those who don't know basic Bible stories because they never crack over their Bible. If that's you, just say "ouch" and keep reading. Haman tries to kill Mordecai, but Esther and her people fast for (3) days. They eventually flip the script on Haman and the gallows set to hang Mordecai were used to kill Haman, and the Jews were victorious at the end.

The moral of the story is, always be grateful for what you have and don't spend your entire life obsessing over what you don't have; it could literally cost you your life. I wanted to share this Lil Bible story because many of us have haters and people that literally have spent a lifetime antagonizing us, and assuming they always had the upper hand on us. Oh, but like the good Father Jesus is, He always allows an opportunity for our enemies to see us win before their very eyes.

See, this is what happened the day I ran into my rapist ten years later. For years I couldn't tell the full story about my rape until today. I always got choked up or I never wished to talk about the full details concerning my rape. A few months after he raped me, I ended up running into him at a poetry show. This is why I hate the fact that St. Louis is so small. The day I saw him, I went into an instant anxiety attack and started panicking. I remember not being able to breathe and my fellow poets were trying to figure out what was going on. After some time, I was finally able to mouth to them, "There is my rapist, the guy who raped me," pointing to the individual across the room. As you can imagine, the brothers wanted to kill him, but I didn't want anyone going to jail on my account. That was the last time I saw him until the Lord led me to Walmart on a random Thursday. You see, at that time, I was homeless and living with a fellow church member. Shoot, I still am as I write this book on a sunken air mattress...I'm just too lazy to inflate it. Well, I needed to get another copy of the house key made, so I decided to go to Walmart. The odd thing about my visit was nothing happened like it should that day. See, I should have originally gone to the Walmart on West Florissant, but I didn't. This one would have been closer to my house. Instead, I ended up on the one on Hanley Road in Brentwood.

I kept asking God why I am coming to this Walmart; nothing about this is convenient. So as I'm copying the house key at one of those key making machines, which I thought was cool by the way because it cut down the wait time of the old fashion way of copying keys and the way my patience was set up it was perfect for me. So, as I was retrieving my new copied key out of the machine, I looked up, and who do I see? My rapist. Now, I'm bad with names and remembering dates, but I never forget a face, especially someone who raped me! He still looked the same except tired in the face, and like life had been beating the crap out of him. I also noticed he was with a woman with a child. I assumed the baby was his, and by their body language, it confirmed that it was.

I thought to myself... I wonder if she would still choose to have a baby by him if she knew her baby daddy was a rapist. Regardless, I felt sorry for him, and as I left the store, a thought crossed my mind. I was no longer afraid of him; I mean, I didn't have a panic attack in the middle of Walmart.

I didn't pause and start pointing in a frantic. I was calm, observant, and even more, I felt in control as I walked through Walmart's parking lot as God revealed to me, "See you no longer have to be afraid, Nicole. I have healed you from the hurt he caused you." Instantly I started smiling and laughing like Will Smith in the midst of the crowd in the movie "Pursuit of Happiness." The sun felt good as it bathed on my face, and so did my new confidence. That is the story of the day I reunited with my rapist.

I felt this story was needed and even important to include in the book because so often, most people don't get to feel what I felt that day in Walmart's parking lot. Shoot, some people may not even believe that this sort of healing is possible. Most have convinced themselves that they just have to walk around with this trauma and learn how to navigate through life with it. I want to encourage you, the reader, that God is a healer and even the sickest, disgusting, and horrendous sexual assaults you can get a pass! You don't have to wear the "victim" like some badge of honor or scarlet letter. It may take some time to get there, but it is possible. I am not healed from all my trauma just yet, but man, am I looking forward to the day when I can say that I am.

BLACKNESS IS
NOT ABOVE THERAPY

y decision to go to therapy was not only for myself but also for the people that refused to go. You see, trauma doesn't just impact you personally, but it also impacts your children and loved ones. Transgenerational epigenetics inheritance states our grandparents' and parents' experiences and trauma can be passed down to future generations through epigenetic tags.

Martha Henriques states in her blog, " Can the legacy of trauma be passed down the generations?" that, "Many of the times when trauma is to have echoed down the generations via epigenetics in humans are linked to the darkest moments in history. Wars, famine, and genccide are all throughout, and have left an epigenetic mark on the descendants of those who suffered them."

So, could the same not be said or applied to African Americans as well? I mean, we are, in fact, mostly all direct descendants of the transatlantic slave trade. The refusal to heal and work on one's own healing journey further perpetuates the theory, "Hurt people, in fact, do hurt people..."

See, our blackness does not make us immune to trauma; it also doesn't negate the fact that we need therapy just as much as any other race. I can't tell you how many times I have witnessed trauma not dealt with but played out in parenting styles in my own family. One time I recall my cousin yelling at her kids while I was visiting. She yelled into the other room, " Sit your ass dcwn somewhere you are always doing something, dang, you get on my nerves." I don't know why, but this statement bothered me so much and even triggered me at that moment. How many times have you witnessed a young mom yelling at her kids for simply just being kids? These moments are products of stress, trauma, and even underlying issues individuals have within their own selves. Children should never consider being cussed at as a replacement of discipline or normalcy because it isn't !! However, for years somehow, our culture has just accepted this behavior and passed it alone as okay.

We also tend to overlook and shun those who speak out against pedophile behavior in the family. As if they are in the wrong for uncle or grandpa touching them all those years. Grandma rather protect her brother that has touched on everyone in the family than admit he has a problem and needs some help. Like really, why do we spend years protecting family secrets and the dirt that is done in the shadows? Doing so only translates to the victim that their voice does not matter. What is the need of telling Keisha to put some more clothes on? Why? When certain family members in the house can't prevent uncle Leroy from looking at her inappropriately. Besides, grown men should never be turned on by the body of an adolescent that's not quite developed, and still a teen!

Lastly, we have to quit sweeping under the rug hypermasculinity and misogyny behavior exhibited by our sons. This behavior shouldn't be tolerated, celebrated, or encouraged for that matter. We place way too much emphasis on little girls being kept and being perfect. We police women about their bodies and what they wear, but in all realness, we should be demanding a standard of all men to keep their hands to themselves and to know that at any time during sex, "No!" simply means no. Rape that happens to any gender, woman or man, is wrong! Also, men can be raped just as well as women. I am holding us accountable to create safe places for our brothers to discuss their trauma, instead of trying to take away the validity of their story simply because of their gender!

In closing, black people, we need therapy, and our BLACKNESS does not make us immune to the impact of trauma. Unhealthy coping mechanisms don't wash away the root of the problem; they only make it worse. Let's start making therapy look cool like we promote Jordan's, mumble rappers, and the latest trend of fashion. Due to the refusal of our parents dealing with their mess is now impacting our generation who chooses mental peace over anything. And we refuse to stay on a stressful job for 10-20 years that won't value our worth or have us growing grey hairs before our time...I'm just saying.

I WAS RAPED,
BUT I'M STILL A VIRGIN!

don't remember exactly how old I was when my grandmother encouraged me to get a pap smear. I do know that it had to be a year or even a few months after I had been raped because the act was still fresh in my mind. You see, I never told anyone in my family that I was raped except for my brothers. They were like my best friends at that time, my Lil protectors and keepers of all my secrets.

Nevertheless, I guess my granny had figured I was having sex by now and encouraged me to go get checked out. You see, I never had a rape kit done on me that night because I threw away the evidence in the dumpster. I also had never been to the doctor or was checked out afterward. So, you can only imagine I was terrified. I often told myself what if I had AIDS, HIV, or some other kind of incurable STD, then what would I do? My little mind just couldn't handle so many unanswered questions, so I just avoided that place.

The weather was cold and gloomy on the day I visited the People's Clinic on Delmar for my pap smear. The nurse that took my initial vitals and information prior to seeing the doctor was ignorant, unprofessional, and rude to me. At one time, she asked me if I had ever been sexually active, and, of course, I paused and replied, "Yes, but no, see it's complicated." I told her I had been raped, so I guess, yes. This lady had the nerve to insinuate that I was lying and even asked me aggressively, "Well, which one is it, Yes or No, Ms. Nelson?"

This lady took one look at me and placed a stereotype on what she assumed I was. I mean, I was 20 something years old and I had to be sexually active, right? At least most women my age were. Well, when the doctor came into the room, she asked me to sit on this cold table. She checked my breast for lumps and even showed me how to do a breast exam on myself. It felt weird to touch my own body because the only time I touch it in any kind of intimate way is in the shower. And no, I'm not referring to masturbation; get your mind out the gutter and stay focused. I'm a poet, so I tend to be overly deep in how I explain things. Well, the doc told me to spread my legs and went to put the clear device in my vagina. I remember I felt a breeze down there and awkward. She assured me she would be gentle and even used this special lubricant. Well, I guess after me screaming a few times when she had barely touched me caused her to never get anywhere with the pap smear, so, she just stopped.

The doctor, a very kind and young African American woman, looked me in my eyes and began to ask me some questions. She asked me if I was raped, and I said yes. She then asked me if the hymen was ever broken? With embarrassment in my eyes, I put my head down and said, I think so. I mean, there was a lot of blood down their doc and pain after the event. So, I assumed he broke it. Long story short, the doctor told me sometimes blood can be produced through rough sex and even a simple tear down there. This doesn't necessarily mean and in the case of me that the hymen was broken.

See, the body has a way of protecting itself. So, when I was being raped because of the aggressive nature of the act and my inability to get wet down there, some tearing occurred.

The doctor went on to say that it is her medical opinion that my hymen is still intact, which explains why the pap smear was so painful for me or well, the one that never happened. The words of that gynecologist echoed in my mind for years to come. To this day, I always paused when people ask me how I am still a virgin when I've been raped. I guess they just assume I adopted the title due to the fact that my 1st time wasn't consensual. The topic itself is a complicated one, but you have to admit it further speaks to the awesomeness of how great God is. The enemy may have stolen something emotional from me, but the physical is still intact!! Excuse me while I pause this book and run around the church and shout on the beat!

Okay, I'm back y'all. This is usually the part where the old folks would say, what the enemy meant for evil; God meant for good. This saying was also an actual scripture to Genesis 50:20 when Joseph assured his brothers after selling him that God allowed it to happen to save his people!

I AM A PRODUCT OF

I spent a great portion of my life preaching, rallying behind, and even advocating for abortion under the circumstances of rape. See, I don't believe in abortion, but I always said rape was the exception to the rule. I had actually convinced myself that even the holiest, radical, and mature Christian surely God could forgive if they aborted under these circumstances. In my mind, I had given this situation the permanent loophole to my stance on pro-choice. This disposition allowed me for years to navigate around such a touchy subject matter and even have others stand in agreement with my stance. Little did I know an accident that God allowed to happen would forever change and challenge my opinion on this.

Do you remember when I told you about a poet named Lightning who encouraged me to write about my rape experience? Well, shortly after I wrote the poem "it wasn't his choice," I became passionate about empowering other women who had similar stories like mine. So, I threw all my energy into dialing up any shelter, group home, and non-profit organization I came across in the phone book. Yes, I said the phone book because, at that time, people were still using these thick books called the Yellow Pages. Crazy, I know, in a world where we depend so heavily on the search engine called Google.

My God-sister and I spoke at several women shelters and led workshops that empowered women that had been abused, raped, and assaulted. I wanted women to know that just because you had been raped, it wasn't the end of the world. In fact, God could heal and give you back your voice through writing. These women would always come up to me after a workshop and thank me for my time. They bragged about how I could be doing anything else with my time because I was so young. Little did they know those encounters with women that looked like me was slowly giving me back my power; the power I felt I had lost on the day that I was raped. But even with all the workshops and speaking engagements, this still wasn't enough for me. I wanted to record a cd, so I set out to record my best poems ever written in the basement of a local rapper in the neighborhood. In that basement with horrible sound equipment, foam padding, and a Radio Shack mic, I recorded my debut album "I am Me." I made sure that "It wasn't his choice" made it on the cd as well. I sampled a song by Destiny Child called "Stand Up for love" as my inspiration in the placement of the poem and recorded the hardest poem I ever wrote in tears.

Well, it would be just my luck that my mother, like any other proud parent, kept begging me on when she would get a copy of my cd. I had made up in my mind to give her the edited version minus the cussing and track 7, the poem about my rape, but in a hurry, I gave her the wrong cd. An hour later, my mother called me and asked me the hardest question in my life. She says, "Track seven, is that you, Nicole?" I swallowed my spit and responded reluctantly; yes, mom, that's me. Knowing I couldn't lie to the prophet or to the woman who God had given dreams of all my Lil business down through the years. Besides, my mother always told me I was never a good liar. So, you see, it was only right that a decade later, those same words would cultivate one of my best attributes, which is integrity. Thanks, momma, your words and access in the spiritual realm did that!

As I stood on the other end, silent, the next thing my mother would say to me, nothing in life could ever prepare me! She goes on to say, " Well, I too had a similar experience happen to me." Confused as to what my mother was referring to, I just kept listening. She tells me that my father told her on her sixteen birthday he would get her pregnant. Pretty much in so many words insinuating on the real story to how I came about. You know how they say there are always three sides to a story. What happened, the truth, and what really happened.

For years it had been whispered and even said my mother was pregnant with me at 15 and had me at sixteen. It seems everyone had their own opinion on my mother's truth and how it all went down. I have even witnessed some use this story to tear down her character and even attack the very essence of what my mother stands for. It seems like whenever this statement would come up, it was always followed with. See, Erica isn't as saved and holy as you would think she is.

Now I know what you are thinking right about now. That it isn't my business to spill my mother's tea, but what you don't know is this, I can't even imagine how many years she held on to that secret! I also can't imagine how she would go on to have a 2nd child by the same man that violated her. I guess this is the part when an old head would chime in and say, love will cause you to do some crazy things. I am convinced I would have never known my mother's story about how I really got here had it not been for that careless mistake on my behalf. In some way, I guess my mother just wanted to relate to me and let me know I wasn't alone in my trauma...sometimes I just wish that it didn't come out like the way it did. The fact, that I found out four months after my own rape that I too was a product of rape, that truth is one I've had a hard time swallowing for some time now. I thought many days long and hard on confronting my dad, but I'm pretty sure I would probably just be more traumatized after the fact.

Not a day goes by that I doubt my dad didn't love my mother, but he also didn't have rights nor access to her simply because she was his girlfriend at the time. Besides, he was several years older than her!! So surely, he should have been able to practice some kind of restraint! After having and knowing this knowledge, I'm not really sure about my stance now concerning pro-choice.

A girl that once preached abortion is now okay in the case of rape after second-guessing that opinion. My former Pastor and spiritual father in the gospel, Joe L. Middleton, always use to say we don't get to dictate how we enter this world. Just know that God makes no mistake. I am the prime example that if my mother had aborted me, my ministry and the ways God has used me the past ten years would not exist. Also, the people impacted by my ministry may not have ever come to know Jesus. Although this topic makes me feel very uncomfortable and angry, I guess in a way; I thank God, nevertheless. For those who are family and may be reading this portion of the book. Let me give you a little piece of advice, keep your mouth off my mother! The only people that really know what went down that day are my mother and father, and I choose to rock with my mother on this one! Lastly, Psalm 105:15 warns us to, "Touch not his anointed and do his prophet no harm."

God is very clear on the repercussions we may have to deal with spiritually when we place our mouth on the people of God, and that's all I have to say on that matter. I don't have the courage yet to discuss this topic in therapy with my therapist because I always tend to deviate from it. Hopefully, one day though, I will have the courage to dive into this Rubik Cube of my existence. Until then, this section will stand as a testament that I am willing to take steps to head in the right direction of that hard conversation.

With that being said, I want to share with the readers a poem that is so appropriate for this section in the book. I wrote it at a time I felt I was so misunderstood about how I loved people and communicated.

MY THOUGHTS (2-5-2010)

I am more complicated than a Rubik cube, crossword puzzles, and a gay catholic priest.

An emotional reck who views on sex has been f**cked up even before my rape.

Can't tell even to this day if my relationship with my father is the reason why I just can't get it right with the men in which I date.

So afraid of being judged by the world, so I continue to hide behind this good girl image.

Be reading scriptures daily in hopes that my sins be forgiven, and my faith be replenished!

You see, I am the queen of misunderstood and despite my intentions to do good.

Lately, people's look and actions towards me makes me question if I even should air out my dirty laundry.

Mother calls me selfish and even stingy at times, at the fact I just want to be able to call something all mine.

Been told that I give many hugs and show too much love when it comes to people.

You see, some mistake my actions for being gay as if when did it EVER become a crime to show loved one or even a friend affection.

Folks don't know that with every hug I give out, It's me only trying to work on my own imperfections.

Cause and effect of a young girl not being shown enough affection when she was young.

So afraid of failure, so I hide behind a wall full of excuses.

My own self-pity replies as to why I can't and cannot do this.

Why I should and did go through this?

Fam still doesn't understand this poetry thing I do even after a dream deferred.

They feel like if I ain't making no Maya Angelou loop, then I'm just another nigga with a pipe dream too.

Fingers stay crossed, four-leaf clover around my neck all while clicking my heels like Dorothy cause I'm gone try every good luck concoction & spell there is

In order to move out from my grandparents' crib and be able to stand on my own two feet.

Everything it requires to make it in this biz,

I am...

More complicated than a Rubik cube, crossword puzzles, and a gay catholic priest.

And the only reason i wrote this poem was because someone rubs me the wrong way today.

And because of my appearance, they figured I wasn't gone have anything to say.

ꟼT WASN'T HIS CHOICE (8-12-09)

It wasn't his choice as he continued to ignore her request of "NO."

All while trying to explore that which she had below.

You see, she had planned this night out in her head a million times before.

She envisioned rose petals, vanilla-scented candles, bubble baths all w/the mix of her favorite slow jam cd.

And her king saying this phrase, baby, I'm so glad you chose me.

Though never did what was supposed to be her perfect night.

Include blood-stained draws with salt like tears all produced by the thing in which she most feared, rape.

It wasn't his choice...

To take her innocence and pride all for a quick ride because too many times before had he been told "no."

Told "NO" that she wanted to wait for her perfect mate, a man sent from God.

A man of faith.

Told "No" because she wasn't just some one-night stand hit it and quit it type of chick.

She had waited 20 something years for this.

And her body had always been her temple.

So, no pants hanging, want to be thug, can't take home to your momma.

Only idea of real goals was getting "MONEY."

She could never allow tasting her forbidden fruit.

And the sweet nectar he desired like all men before him.

But still, it wasn't his choice...

To pen her to the bed, then begin to tug back and forth with her while she pleaded

with him for him not to undo her threads.

But you see, the idea that she was someone's daughter had to escape his mind.

All while he threw her pants across the room.

Cause it mattered more to him to please the urges of his hormones.

Then to answer to the cries of her "NO" please stop, please don't do this!

See, never could you imagine just how dirty she feels.

See that bus ride home appeared to be the loneliest and longest ride of her life.

Cause now her heart is filled with nothing but hatred, confusion, and fear.

Fear of how she could ever look her mother in the face and tell her earlier that day, her baby had been raped.

You see, she was trying to muster up the strength to stop crying.

Cause people on the bus began to talk, ask questions, even look at her funny.

And the bus driver even asked, " Aye Lil momma..., you aight".

Not once, never looking up to show her face, arms folded crisscross to hide her tears, she replied, yes.

But see what they didn't know is 20 min ago, in a bathroom downstairs, she wiped the blood from her vaginal area down there.

And in a scream so loud that the neighbor could hear.

I'm bleeding; she cried in despair.

See, because it wasn't until two weeks ago a conversation, she had w/ a friend name Kristy.

Did she have to digest that Lil miss innocent four months ago was a rape victim?

And it doesn't matter how many times she plays in the back of her mind the situation of her attack on that day. And it doesn't matter that she tries to block out that she was wearing her favorite black skinny jeans. White tee, red & blue denim Jordan shoes.

All that match her favorite fur coat jacket.

Cause you see this fool had told her the way she looked in those skinny jeans was just a tease.

But still, it's not a day that doesn't go by that she isn't reminded that it wasn't his choice to take that from me, my v.i.r.g.i.n.i.t.y

FOLLOW YOUR DREAMS...

It's a hard pill to swallow when you realize the bulk of your writing is the byproduct of all the trauma you've been through. As I explore the pages of my old notebooks decorated with yellow tint, rips and tears, visible signs that show the proof of the age of some of these poems and the fact many are holding on by a thread in my notebook. I can't help but perplex that the girl that once wrote all these things is me and a younger version of myself. I am reminded of all my frustrations, lack of access to a network, and stubborn- ness to hold on to the idea that I am someone great even if I have to fight past my own insecurities and ignorance of those around me.

You see, poetry wasn't the only way I tackled my depression, I love to paint and go to parks. There was always this neighborhood park right next door to my old elementary school that I went to in order to clear my head. I would spend hours walking and talking to myself. Yelling to the heavens as if someone or something would respond back to me. No one ever did, and I'm pretty sure it was because I was filled with way too much anger.

In my grandmother's home, we had a basement that had an additional little storage room built by the previous owners. It wasn't anything fancy, but a door rigged to close and a room encompassed with a few wooden shelves. We pretty much used this room to store Christmas decorations and anything else the family needed to store but refused to organize or sort through it. The room had everyone's stuff including mine, Aunt Shari, Angelo, grandma, and papa. What my grandparents didn't know was on days they were not there, I would go downstairs and break things like glass, poetry, or anything I could get my hands on.

Eventually, I realized how foolish it was to keep breaking my things, so I started taking my anger out on my scooter helmet. I mean, I would take this thing downstairs and just go crazy on those cement walls. I would bang and cuss until I grew tired and there was no more strength left.

I was angry with God at this time because of my life.

I was angry that I wasn't in college like my friends.

I was angry that I felt stagnant in my poetry career.

Let's just say I was angry and depressed with the world.

Well, one day, I realized my anger was counter-productive, and I needed someone to see and know what I was going through. I got tired of hiding in the shadows. So,I asked my granny one summer if I could paint my walls. Not fully grasping what I was asking her, she said, " Sure, we can always just paint over the walls." I was ecstatic and ran to Home Depot immediately, bought some acrylics and brushes, and began my mural.

This mural would be a testimony that my depression was real, and everything I went through. I would spend hours in that room, just painting. Some of my family would come over to see what I was doing in that room and even the neighbors. Some even asked me why I wrote such things as "Follow your dreams," then crossed it out with yellow tape. The truth was I used that mural to say everything I was too afraid to put into words. I painted until I became bored with the project and felt I had nothing else left to say.

To this day, that mural still sits in my grandparents' house. They never did paint over those walls. But every time I see it, I know that my depression and experiences were real. Most importantly, I know that at a time I should have broken, I didn't!

A Dream Deferred (05-14-09)

Someone, please tell me exactly what is a dream deferred.

Is it that which Langston Hughes once spoke of before he died?

Or maybe it was the people of Katrina who was told they should continue to hold their heads up high.

After they were forced for days to sit upon rooftop w/SOS signs, sheet covers as they watch their loved ones die.

See, even though these are great examples of a dream deferred.

I poetic-one am an example of a dream being deferred each and every day.

Having to diagnose me w/this hater mentality.

Since I got stuck w/three kids, let me shatter your dreams, Nicole.

That the idea of making it in this poetry game is nothing but a bullsh*t dream of reality

Reality being that if I make straight A's in school.

The next thing following this should be college after high school.

See if I had a $1 for every time I was told thatI was too smart not to be in school.

Then I guess I would be rich.

See, there would no longer be a need for me to spit these words of conviction.

Cause never could you understand like that crackhead w/that itch.

Even if you surgically removed P.O.E.T.R.Y from me.

It's something that can't be fixed.

See before poetic-one was thought of, God birthed Nicole to do this.

Loved ones, those in who I was often told should have my back.

Have the audacity to tell me I need to go get a real job.

Yet I can't remember the last time or if you came to a show!

Cause if you did, you would understand that by asking me to settle for a regular 9-5.

It's like telling me just to lay ova and die.

See, I understand at the age of 20; one should have achieved acar and be working towards a degree.

Cause this to society is what they judge me upon.

As if in life, I will go far.

But see, you got to understand that I tithe and give poetry my last $5 like it was a religion itself; Metro linking and busing it.

So Soul Sessions, Soul Stage, and Legacy if this ain't dedication.

Then me up here, faithfully spitting my soul, is a figment of your imagination.

So, let me ask you again.

What exactly is a dream deferred?

Cause the next time you tell me that I can't do poetry for a living.

I guess poets such as Saul Williams, Nikki Giovanni, Gill Scott Heron, The Last Poets, Langston H., And Maya Angelou you ain't ever heard.

So, every time you tell me that poetry ain't a real job.

Remember this; you are contributing to my dream being deferred.

PATTERNS

It would be unfair of me to insinuate or blame all my trauma on others and family. When I know, I have done a great dealing of contributing to my trauma too! You see, I contributed through my poor choice of men. For some odd reason, I went through a period of being attracted to bad boys in my teens and inconsistent men in my 20's. These men were the type that was slick with their words, pretty boys, musicians, and poets. They all had something in common with the ability to string me along for years or play me like a fiddle. It had even got to a point I began to give them nicknames and even serial date men in my teens. I convinced myself that this allowed me to be in charge of my own destiny. Men this way would not be able to play me, but I played them. Man, that was short-lived, that was a lie I sold to myself.

Let me tell you how I met mister "In and Out" is what I called him. In and out was tall, slender, with a great sense of fashion and a glorious beard! I mean, it used to always smell like coconut oil and was never nappy like pubic hairs that sit on some men's faces, never to see the light of a comb or clippers. He always smelled good too! We had met at a poetry show at a local church. The funny thing was that I wasn't even supposed to be there that night. However, a fellow poet had offered to give me a ride, and I ended up in attendance. After performing, as I was selling my CDs, he asked me if that was my number on the back. I assured him that it was, in fact, my real contact number, but I was too slow to catch the hint that dude was trying to holla. I gave him a free cd and went about my business. The following morning, he hit me up on FB and asked me out on a date.

I will never forget his approach; It was so old skool, timid, and cute. He mentioned how he hoped he wasn't being too forward because he wasn't sure if I was taken and if he could take me out. If I knew at the time years later, that he would be the living embodiment of Lauryn Hill's song "Ex-factor," I would have run towards the hills and never looked back. His love was toxic, frustrating, draining, and exhilarating all at the same time! At the time, he was my drug of choice! We went on the following week a series of 10 dates. It was some of the best times of my life. He took me to Dave & Buster, Boston Market, Market Pub, and several other places. I was hooked, y'all and every single day following our initial date, this man was taking up all my time, but I didn't mind! I loved the way he smelled, and my God, that beard was sexy! Unfortunately, In and Out came into my life at a horrible time! You see, in the following two weeks, I was moving to Vegas to be with my God-sister, and I had already booked a 1-way ticket. So, me and Mr. In and out could never be. I remember asking him to drive me to the airport, and he refused, saying he couldn't say goodbye to the woman he had felt so hard for, and my baby brother Nino took me instead.

I should have just ended it there, but noo, my hopeless romantic self-convinced dude that we could do a long-distance relationship! Big mistake; after a few months in Vegas, I ended up homeless, living in a women's shelter, and In and Out became my daily headache. The dude actually blamed me for being homeless. He also blamed me for not giving more to our relationship despite my crazy circumstances at the time. Frustrated and feeling over-whelmed, I broke it off. I couldn't be in a healthy relationship and homeless at the same time. Besides, the dude was stressing me all the way out! Months later, I moved back to St L. and crazy me assumed we could work it out.

Maybe I was trying to relive those passionate first ten dates, or maybe I was desperate who knows. However, he had relocated to Ohio and blamed me for his leaving, so we spent the next five years in this back and forth thing. At times he would be in a relationship, and I would be single and vice versa. He always complained about everything I did. He was a narcissist in his own way, always making me feel bad for his own inability to man up! Then he would manipulate me and tell me he was too good for me, which he was, but like a fool, I kept coming back for more verbal abuse. I talked to this man all the way up until like 2016! I don't know what the breaking point was for me, but I guess I just got tired of his games. Over the years, he wasn't as cute to me as the day we met. His behavior and treatment began to overshadow the mystique that caused me to be so obsessed with him in the first place.

His slender body became a slight pudge, and evidence of him eating good, the fly haircut hairline slowly began to recede. I mean, dude was in doubt about losing his hair, obviously. I still think about In and Out from time to time and what could have been. I even get random impulses to check his FB page even though social media was never his thing. I don't know why a part of me still holds on to something so toxic. But he is just one guy among many that I created soul ties with. In and out, if you are reading this, let the lining go, baby, and just rock a bald haircut. Besides, you still have one of the best beards I know. Oh, and get some therapy, boo! You're a great guy, but your own trauma tends to self-sabotage any woman that tries to get close to you.

The next toxic man that I'm going to talk about never got a cute Lil nickname from me, but the man did do a number on me too. Let's just call him Freckles, the artist. Freckles and I met in high school because his cousin was dating my friend at that time, Camille. He was a high yellow, scrawny, pretty boy too. As you can see, I clearly had a type! When I first met him, he was sweet, shy, and timid. He never tried to bust a move on me because he was just too shy for that. Over the years, we kept in contact after high school. He went off to college, graduated, and got his degree in graphic design, I believe. Freckles was brilliant, well-spoken, articulate, creative, and there was something about his eyes. We never ended up in a relationship, but God knows he and I tried several times. It was just like in the beginning; time was never on our side.

When Freckles moved to Chicago, we were both single. I, at the time, was living in a cute Lil apartment on Michigan in the hood, and from the outside, my place looked like the project, but on the inside, it was like its own oasis. With plants, a mattress on the floor, and a cute living room set paired with a flat screen tv. We spent hours talking on the phone and making plans on how we were going to make us finally work. Does this sound familiar?? Freckles was a YouTuber and a savvy entrepreneur, but like other toxic men, he had ways about himself too. He would string my own broken promises, and despite his ambition in his career, he never applied the same amount of effort to us. He placed so much emphasis on our childhood past that he felt he never had to put forth much effort.

Eventually, I grew tired of his broken promises and the stories he painted of us being together that appeared he wasn't doing the work to make it happen. In frustration, I told Freckles to either put in work or leave me alone. When he finally moved to STL. I thought, finally, it was our chance to be together. This time people and distance would no longer get in our way. But in Freckle's typical fashion, he only put out the bare minimum effort towards us. When we met again, he had put on some weight and also grown out his hair and started locking. I always hated locs on him because he used being an entrepreneur as an excuse to stay groomed, and not get locs. Secretly I wished he would just cut that mess! He was always trying to talk me into retwisting his hair too. What once went from admiration for the businessman, quickly turned into resentment on my behalf. I resented him because, as Lauryn Hill said, it could all be so simple, but he always made it hard when it came to us!

I saw greatness in him, and somehow, he always managed to make me feel like he considered me as a second option. Freckles eventually ended up getting some other woman pregnant. This pissed me off because, of course, he would perpetuate a good man getting a hoe pregnant stereotype. The baby mother was something else too. After this news, I definitely couldn't take him seriously. The mother of his child was legit a one-night stand or woman he didn't take seriously, to say the least. This fool even had the nerves to tell me he wanted to marry me and wanted us to be cool, referring to the mother of his child. Well, eventually,

I resented Freckles so much and my ability to just allow him to come in and out my life with no consistency. So, I gathered the strength to block and delete him on FB. I knew by doing this, I could finally move on from his toxic ways. I'm just sad it took me over eight years to gather the courage to set boundaries with this man. We would never get married. He would never stop making excuses, and I refuse to be someone's option. So, Freckles, if you manage to get a hold of this book, the next dope woman that comes your way. Just do the work, Love. You have so much potential to be a great man like the great father you already are.

The last man I want to talk about is my friend who I nicknamed Keith Sweat. This was because he, too, was a pretty boy that looked like one of those guys from the 90s on the cover of a bomb cd. I mean, he definitely would be the type to sing in the rain like Ray J's "One wish" video or wear the famous turtleneck sweater. I met Keith Sweat through my childhood friend Breia. We were all having lunch in the loop, and I had no idea he would be joining us. Keith's Sweat was fine! He was athletic, about 5'9, rocked a low haircut, with what I remember as a great athlete butt! Don't judge me because you know the type I'm talking about.

From the moment I met him, I wanted him to be mine so much, so the 1st time we all hung out bowling, I made sure to let my intentions be known. At the time, he was in a relationship, but it was struggling, of course. I made up in my mind that if she didn't know how to treat him well, I did. Big mistake, old girl probably would have told me to run towards the hills and save myself some energy and three years of heartbreak. Ladies never believe a guy when they wish to dog a woman and place the blame of the failed relationship all on her. Chances are he's a dog just trying to make himself look better.

So that struggling relationship didn't last as I assumed. That night we exchanged numbers after bowling, and shortly after they broke it off, we were an item. I was madly in love with Keith Sweat. I mean, I thought I was in love within and out, but that was just an infatuation. At least that's what I thought. He was the type of man that would cause me to be all types of stupid for him. Fresh into our relationship, he cheated on me with this random girl at a party. This negro had the nerves to sleep with her and then was mad that my girl told me all the details, like did he really think my homegirl would allow me to be in the streets looking stupid? Oh, and the plot thickens...That same girl he cheated on me with almost had sex with my homegirls' older brother but passed out drunk. And like the saint that I was at the time, what do I do? I helped the poor child out. I helped the homewrecker not choke on her own vomit, and it was everywhere on that basement floor. I helped change her clothes and made sure she was treated with dignity.

Well, the story got back to Keith Sweat, who had taken it upon himself to break up with me after cheating on me. Can you believe it? He went on about how cool of me that was to do it. He even questioned how I could be so nice to her, considering the circumstances. I told him I was a classy lady, and that's how I'm still going to talk to him after his cheating. I told you I was stupidly in love with him. He was the 1st man feet I ever rubbed and after the fact, he accused me of doing this for other men. He said I was so good at it that surely this wasn't my 1st time. That remark angered me, and I rejected Keith sweat; he didn't deserve my bomb foot rub with shea butter and love! Shoot, I put all kinds of great energy into that foot rub. Ladies, this is what happens when you give husbands' benefits to men who don't deserve it.

I spent three years exactly trying to get over that man. I cried over him several times and wrote countless poems about him, including my famous poem, " I would love to get lost in you." It seems like the poems didn't help, but just further feed his ego that I would always wait on him like some stray puppy. Eventually, he got a woman pregnant, and when I found out, it broke something inside of me. I remember him telling me that if the baby was his, he would do right by her and take care of it. Well, he kept his promise and married that woman. They now have beautiful kids and left me to wonder why I couldn't be the woman to have his kids. I was supposed to lose my virginity to him, and I had planned it all out. It was supposed to be his Christmas present. My friend told me what condoms to buy and all, and I also made him show me proof of being tested. I was naive, but not that dumb. I often feel like that was God saving me from having further soul ties with that man. If I gave him my cookies, I would have been messed up for life! I also would have taken longer than three years to get over him.

I WOULD LOVE TO GET LOST IN YOU

I would love to get lost in you.

I'm talking amber alert, milk carton, and never be found.

Be so high spiritually connected no marijuana needed that we never come down.

Just get temp amnesia in order that I could learn you all over again.

Go blind in order that I would feel you deeper.

Lose my legs in order that we, you, could carry our love always.

LIVING WITH IT IS TOO LONG
TO SPELL...SYRINGOHDROMYELIA

magine you are having one of the most awesome days of your life. I mean, if I had to rate my positivity, surely, it was a 20 on this particular day. I had just landed a job at Dollar Tree, which was conveniently right up the street just like I prayed for. Also, my disability appointment was the following day, so I could finally have some extra cash flowing in. It seemed like God had finally started answering my Lil prayers, or so I thought.

Later that night, I went into the kitchen to grab something, knowing me it was probably a Lil snack to suffice my sugar craving. Pray for me, saints because I rebuke diabetes, but I love chocolate, chips, and cakes! As I was heading out, the lady I was staying with asked me what was going on with that job I was supposed to start. I don't know why, but this statement not only angered me, but it also triggered me.

I often wished I could find the words to formulate to express to her that living with mental illness is HARD WORK! Most days, I have to conquer just wanting to wash my own butt or even get out the bed. Such good days like this particular day don't come often. However, I couldn't expect her to understand something I was never willing to share or disclose. Some days I just wished she would discover I was on medication for depression, PTSD and anxiety, or even the Lord should show it to her in a dream.

I secretly believe, I left my bedroom door open for this purpose on many of days. I just wanted to tell her so badly what I was suffering from in silence, but Jesus never released me to do so. So, this often made for a disconnect in our communication. After her comment was made, something triggered in my brain, and the next thing I know, I went into an all-out panic attack. I remember exhibiting signs of paranoia 1st. I kept pacing the floor, breathing heavily, and talking to myself. I called my spiritual Godmother and told her what was going on. She began to talk me through my panic attack, but things only progressed and became worse. At one point, I kept telling her the walls were closing in on me, and I had to get out of this house. She asked me if I had taken my medication yet, and reluctantly, I said no. She then told me to take it while I was on the phone with her. It must have taken me over 10 min to take my meds because those voices convinced me in my head not to. After I took my anxiety medication, the situation just escalated. If I wasn't paranoid at 1st now, I was in a mental hospital, straight jacket, and padded room crazy. I paced the floor so much I could have ran a hole into the carpet. Not to mention my little room was no bigger than about two closets in a U. City house. If you are not familiar with these comparisons or measurements, just refer to a fellow U. City person.

My Godmother must have tapped into the spirit of suicide because immediately, she started pleading the blood of Jesus and binding up suicide. Looking back on this, I like to think it was her initial prayer that put a dent into Satan's original plan concerning my life. Eventually, I reached the conclusion that I needed to go to a safe place for the night, and I would go over my Pooh's house or a friend's house who lived downtown. So, after telling my Godmother, she agreed this was a good plan. She even offered to pay for an Uber to take me to my destination. I must have texted over four people that night, asking if I could spend the night at their home, and most either didn't respond or greeted me with way too many questions than what my feeble mind could handle at the time. After texting my pooh back and my homegirl, I just said forget it.

In my mind, anxiety told me no one loved me and definitely didn't care to allow me to spend a night at least. Couldn't they see my cries for help via text? I even told one friend it was an emergency, and I just needed a safe place to stay. After that last text, I ran to FB to vent.

Now pause, I know you are thinking this is a horrible decision Nicole, but honestly, it was my last cry for help as I was delusional at this point. I had long hung up the phone with my Godmother. Two statues I posted was "What do you do when you're feeling suicidal, and people just keep asking you stupid questions?" The second one was " F$ck if. I only wanted a safe place to stay tonight!" after I posted this, people began to flood my inbox on FB and my cell phone with calls. However, it was way too late now. After I posted that status, I had already researched ways to kill myself via medication and the chances of it stopping my heart rate. I laid out on the floor, sitting Indian style, opening both pill bottles, and pouring Zoloft and Hydroxyzine into the tops. By this time, my "sunshine" was blowing my phone up back and forth that we could fix this and to please answer her phone calls. I never did answer her phone calls, but I did text twice, "I loved her." I took over 15 pills of my Zoloft and 2 Hydroxyzine pills. The last thing "sunshine" texted me back before I blacked out was, "Nicole, please don't do this; we can fix this." I texted her back too late. I already took the pills and said, I love you. At this time I'm thinking, Jesus please don't let my black butt die, at least not like this.

My granny always said never end up at the hospital with no clean draws on, and I certainly had the smell of the day on me, and a sister was on her cycle. I needed a hot bath, and some of my favorite body butters before the paramedics were to find me. The last text I sent before I closed my eyes and started foaming in the mouth was to my Godmother. I instructed her to call 911 and that I loved her. I also gave her the address of the home I was staying at. I really didn't want to die that night, but my antidepressant made me suicidal and paranoid. There really was nothing anyone could have said to stop me from killing myself that night. Believe me, many of my friends, family, and even church members tried to call and reach out to me but I ignored every last call.

I never did get around to taking the second top of pills because, honestly, I didn't want them to have to pump my stomach with all those meds. By the time the paramedics had arrived, I was lying on the floor going in and out. They positioned me in a posture so that I wouldn't choke on my own spit. These folks flashed lights all in my pupils and asked me dumb questions like, why did you try to kill yourself, Nicole? To the saint that allowed me to live with her at this time. I am sorry your children had to see me laid out on the floor this way. I am also sorry you had to find out about my mental condition in this kind of way. I wouldn't have wished this image upon anyone. If I could take that night back, I promise I would.

After several questions about rather or not, I could walk, I was taken out on a stretcher. Oh, I forgot to mention it was cold that night and also a really bad snowstorm. All I had on was my Jesus is God hoddie and favorite sweatpants with my tan UGG boats. Why, as to what I was wearing has any relevance to my story I will double back to later on in this chapter.

While in the ambulance, both paramedics were white and ignorant. I don't know if they assumed, I was extremely drugged up or simply just didn't take anything, but they did not attempt to hide their true feelings regarding my incident. The entire ride to the hospital they made comments that nothing was wrong with me, I probably was just faking it, they wished I would turn off my stupid phone, and I seemed to be pretty cognitive to them. I really do hope that if the tables were turned and they were in my shoes that there would be way more compassion and professionalism shown to them than me. I mean, seriously, you really wish my phone would stop ringing because folks are blowing it up because I just OD on my meds. Lord, racism, and ignorance really are rapid in St. LOUIS.

Upon arriving at the hospital, I was greeted with 8 hours of even more ignorance. When I tell you, I am so grateful for people like my Godmother and two God sisters in the medical field, I mean it!! So many people, especially black women, are disregarded and treated poorly in our hospitals and clinics, which is sickening! For years it has been assumed because of our ethnicity that our pain tolerance is higher and that in most cases, we are exaggerating when we mention the symptoms we exhibit while in pain.

The room the hospital put me in must have been the low income special because it had all the bare essentials and screamed, "Nigga, I ain't got no hospital insurance!" I'm just saying this room was smaller than an Arab corner store in the hood, now that is small. Once I was placed on a bed, Becky, the nurse comes in to take off all my clothes. Her name really wasn't Becky, but for the purpose of protecting folks' names, everyone has a silly alias symbolic of their personality. So, what was I saying?Oh yeah, Becky stripped me of all my clothing, and I don't know why this felt so degrading, but the last thing I remember saying to her before being butt naked on that table was. "Wait, wait...I'm on my cycle, and she was like oh, one minute." Becky comes back with this Dollar General depend that looks like a maxi pad, and it was huge as heck!! Becky puts me in these thin paper mesh-like material pants and shirts. I don't know what this material was made out of. Apparently, a Christian Hospital got together, and sone nerd in a lab suggested to give suicide patients these clothes made out of itchy sackcloth and tissue paper. The attire wasn't certainly not fashion forward but had budget cuts and savings in mind.

That night while lying in that small hospital bed, I saw the outline of demons coming toward me and the death angel himself!! I was so afraid because I knew Satan had been trying to kill me for years. I told God, please don't let me die, Lord, at least not like this. The Lord then comforted me and told me to look at the stainless-steel wall on my right. He has, in fact, dispatched Gabriel and Michael on my behalf, and I would not die. I saw these huge two figures of bright light, and instantly I was encouraged. I looked at the demons traveling fast towards me and said, I rebuke you, Satan with the blood of Jesus! It's not my time yet!

It's funny because every time I tell this story, if it had not happened to me, I wouldn't have believed it either. What I am about to say to you next changed my whole outlook on the supernatural and how Jesus works. The night I tried to commit suicide, Jesus had work for me to do, and knowing

Jesus, if he can use a donkey, surely me being high as a kite and barely being able to walk wouldn't stop him either. That night I tried to use the bathroom more than four times. Maybe it was all the meds I took, but my bladder felt super full like I was about to explode. They also had a yellow band on my wrist, which indicated that I was a fall risk. I kept getting out of my bed because I had to pee badly but every single time the ghetto nurses in the front would assist me back to my room, saying I couldn't get up. They also joked about what they would do to me if I got up out of my bed one more time.

Finally, my actual nurse Becky comes back, and I told her I had to pee so badly, so she brought one of those portable toilets to my room to use. My legs were like jello, and I could barely stand, let alone walk more than 2ft. I tried to use that little toilet, but nothing came out. Finally, I told nurse Becky that my bladder was full, but I couldn't pee. She told me if that was the case, she would have to put a catheter in me. If she didn't, the outcome could affect me in a bad way seeing I had not peed in hours. I didn't really know the process for a catheter, but I knew one thing; Becky was not sticking that thing up in my vagina. I remember my homegirl had to get one of those when she was in the hospital and the pain that it caused her. So much pain that her non-verbal self-asked me her friend to just rub the pubic area to relieve some of the tension. Of course, I told her we weren't that close, and that was more of a job for a man to do, so I yelled for him to come into the room and do his manly duties. Lol

At that time, while Becky went to go look for me a catheter to help me pee, I started making promises with Jesus I knew I couldn't keep! I placed my hand over my vagina and commanded my body to pee in Jesus' Name. By faith, I wobbled to my portable potty, waited 20 sec and pee gushed out like a broken fire hydrant nigga rigged for the kids in the summertime. By the time the nurse came back, she was astonished as I pointed to my bedpan full of yellow urine. She asked how I did it and what happened. I told her I didn't want her to stick that thing up in me, so I commanded my body to pee. The nurse was astonished and in utter belief. For over 2 hours, I couldn't pee... now, don't tell me what prayer with a hint of faith won't do in desperate times.

As I sat up in my bed like a nosey grandmother in the living room window, I observed everything around me. Eventually, my eyes zoomed in on a young black nurse around the same age as I was. She couldn't have been any older than 32 at the oldest. I remember waving or saying hi to her, and she smiled back. I think she even asked me if I needed anything. That poor little lady, she has ignored me because the rest of the night for over 5 hours, she heard me call her name without failing. I can still hear my high self-yelling out, " Nurse Tiffany....God has a word for you!". After wondering why I was staring this lady up and down, God laid in my heart to wave her down to come in my room. I don't remember the 1st conversation I had with her, just that she was sweet, and I gave her a mini word. Then I asked her if she knew the young man that took my blood work earlier. She said yes, and I asked her if she could get him for me. Eager, she responded yes and went to search for him on my behalf. After about 15 minutes, the young man appeared.

By this time, the pills I took has really kicked in. I was high as a kite and talking very low like I was 90 years old. I asked the nurse to step closer, so I wouldn't strain my voice and I began to tell him that God had a word for him. I asked him if he was in school for something, and he confirmed yes. I asked if he was taking finals or some kind of exam he was worried about. I told him not to worry that God would give him favor during all his exams and that he would do well. I went on to tell him that he was an overachiever and that he does everything with the spirit of excellence. I told him that this is what also allows him to be good at his work in the hospital. He shook his head in agreement and said yes, ma'am.

The Lord really didn't have a lot to say to him, but more than anything, He wanted me to encourage the young man and let him know that God is concerned with the things that concern him. After leaving my room. I could hear him talking in the room next to me about all I had told him. He told the other nurses how I could have known all that and that I was a prophet. He encouraged them to go into the room. They reluctantly responded that they were not going in that lady room, referring to me. He said it wasn't scary, but that I would just tell them stuff about themselves.

I just laughed at the fact that they didn't know I could hear everything they were saying about me. I guess being on my meds wasn't so bad after all. I got a little humor, a cute nurse to draw my blood, and even got a chance to give a word. Little did I know God still wasn't done with me yet. Oh, this was only the tip of the iceberg. If those nurses thought I was spooky, they had no idea. The things God would ask of me in the next 2 hours would make me the most talked-about patient that night and not in a good way. While I tried to get some rest, Mrs. Inga and Dontae showed up to my surprise. I had so many questions in my mind as she greeted me with that twinkle in her eye, innocent laugh, and the prettiest gap I have ever laid eyes on.

So many unspoken words were written over the face of someone who looked at me as a bonus daughter for years. Inga held my right hand tight under the itchy hospital covers. She constantly rubbed my hand and looked off at a distance as she tried to hide her tears that intercepted her conversation with no warning at all. I will never forget the fear I saw in her eyes that night. If I ever questioned the depth of how much she loved me, God confirmed all my questions as she held my hand at 2 am in the morning. Despite a snowstorm, she asked Dontae to drive her to see little old me. I told her about the death angel and the angels in my room. I also told her I had a word to give to nurse Tiffany.

Inga tried to help me get nurse Tiffany's attention because God wouldn't allow me to go to sleep until I released that word. I also remember saying to Dontae something about God restoring healing in his hands or something like that. He laughed and said, try to get some rest, no more prophesying. I closed my eyes and tried to fall asleep, and Inga and Dontae left. Ten minutes later, I shook my head in agony because God was persistent and meant it when he said I couldn't rest until I released this word to nurse Tiffany. Afterward, Tutu shows up. I don't even know how she found out about me being in the hospital or Inga, for that matter.

Yet here she was in typical Tutu fashion with her black girl scarf, tee-shirt, and yoga pants that screamed I only shop at Nordstrom and Costco! She hugged me and immediately and started going off on the nurses about why they had me looking ratchet. Tutu went into her purse and pulled out wipes, Chapstick, lotion, and I'm pretty sure anything else that helps you navigate through the 1st 24hrs in the emergency room. Next thing I know, this lady is wiping my face down with baby wipes, moisturizing my ashy lips all while fussing at the nurses about why I had hot water in my cup to drink. The Lord knew to send Tutu because she was the one who could get those nurses all the way together. She made sure I had ice chips because I was extremely dehydrated. I also choked on my water several times because I was so thirsty. I also told Tutu about the angels, and how God had sent me to the hospital to do work that night. She just hugged me and said, oh baby, I believe you.

Now, if you have never met Twana Tucker or had the privilege to be in her presence, you are doing life all wrong! She is one of the most professional, bougie, tell it like it is with a Colgate smile even celebs would kill for. Yep, that's my Tutu. Her favorite saying is, "I'm a single momma of two kids, and I ain't got no money." Now despite her declaring this mantra to anyone who will listen, Tutu is far from struggling, and if she is, she makes the struggle look good. I told Tutu the same thing I told Inga and Dontae, and that is the Lord won't allow me to go to sleep until I release this word. Well, in typical Tutu fashion, she made it her mission to hunt this nurse Tiffany down. The poor nurse told her she had other patients and was overwhelmed that night, but she would definitely come to my room when she had some free time.

To this day, I think Tutu threatened that poor nurse. After waiting patiently for about 20 min, nurse Tiffany showed up. I released a word that lasted over 10 min. God had a lot to say to her. He told me it wasn't by mistake that I came to the hospital at the time I did. You see, she was an overnight nurse and had an OD a tad bit earlier and I would have missed her. He wanted me to warn her of gossiping nurses that constantly put their mouth on her because of the favor of God on her life. She confirmed there was, in fact, a nurse that worked at the nurses' station that gossiped a lot. I told her to stay away from that lady. I also told her not to be discouraged in well-doing despite only being one out of two Christians on her floor, and God was well pleased with the work she had been doing and how she treated her patients. Also, Jehovah God wanted me to tell her that His people have been asking to see signs and wonders. Tell them I am the sign and wonder referring to me and what he was allowing to take place in my body.

Once I was done, Nurse Tiffany thanked me, and finally, I was able to sleep. I asked Tutu if she would lay in the bed with me, and she just held me until I fell asleep. I will never forget how Tutu eased all the concerns I had that night. She contacted all my friends on my behalf because they had confiscated my cell phone being on suicide watch and all.

The next day they transferred me to the 2nd floor. My entire time spent at a Christian Hospital was a supernatural experience, and that really is the only way I can describe it. I know this hospital gets a bad rep for poor service, but that never was my experience. From the cleaning staff, nurses, doctors, and med techs, God literally gave me the elite of the hospital. The majority of all my nurses were Christian and extremely polite! For the next couple of days, God ministered to me during my stay. He showed me how angels were still in my room, and this time more than two. He said every time I saw flashes of light, that was the indication they were there, and they watched over me night and day.

The next day my folks came to visit me in the hospital, and according to my best friend Kelly, I was not your typical patient. I was still high on meds and the doctors were still cleaning up all the drugs I had taken. Apparently, I kept whining about needing to take a shower to the nurse and that I needed to wash my twat. I told her my friend Blue was visiting me, and my twat couldn't be stinking. All those meds I had overdosed on were coming out of my system and not agreeing with my ph. balance at the time.

Now you would think after almost dying, I would be more concerned with more pressing matters rather than taking a shower and my twat. However, that wouldn't be true to who I am. Nicole Nelson, despite my medical condition or appearance, cared more about showering, smelling clean, and a balanced ph. balance than all the other medical mumbo jumbo the nurses were talking about.

During my stay at the Christian Hospital, my nurses loved me and called me low maintenance!! I never asked for anything other than water and to shower, and I always thanked everyone who was super polite! Eventually, as I came to myself and was no longer high, I realized something wasn't right about my walking. I was still a BIG fall risk, and my legs could barely stabilize themselves long enough to make it to the toilet. The doctors were also confused and perplexed about what was going on with me. I had a total of three MRI's done on me. Two on my entire body and the last one on my spine. The 1st time I spent 20 minutes in this white tube. I was petrified and scared I would move and have to start the test over again! The doctor gave me headphones and put it on Joy 91.1. The entire time I said quietly to myself, I can do all things through Christ Jesus who strengthens me. Well, I made it through the entire 20 minutes without moving to my surprise. Still, they couldn't figure out what was wrong. The second to last day, they ran one more test on my spine— this time, I had to lay still for a total of 45 minutes. I just knew I would move and start freaking out in that white tube. I repeatedly said I can do all things through Christ Jesus who strengthens me, and I was able to lay still the entire time.

After a few hours, the doctor came to my room to let my mother and I know I had been diagnosed with Syringohydromyelia. The word was so long that we asked her to write it down for us. Apparently, I had a rare condition where fluid was leaking on my spine in the form of a cyst and impacting my nervous system. It caused my body to shake tremendously and impacted my ability to walk. My whole world had been turned upside down at that moment. I went from being able-bodied to now needing a cane or walker to assist me. I now fear steps of any kind, and my legs have given out on me three times so far. My family is extremely overprotective over me and barely allows me to go anywhere alone. I can no longer work, and I am currently waiting for my disability determination as I type this section.

These days I look forward to people visiting me and going to Walmart. On my worse days, I feel angry, frustrated, embarrassed, and uncertain of what the upcoming months look like for me. I now completely rely on the help of those around me for the most basic things, like carrying a glass bowl to the table safely. I hate having to ask folks to cash app me money, which usually occurs every other two days. Thankfully, God has touched several people's hearts that they always bless me with more than I ask for. Of course, I tithe off every cash app I receive too!! Some night I awake to bad shakes in my sleep of my body throwing itself forward.

My worst fear is that I will never be married and that my chances of being in a healthy relationship are really bad now because I'm disabled. I mean, who really would want to willingly take on this. Shoot, I didn't even want to, and it's me! I never take a full body shot on FB, out of fear someone will see my cane or walker. I still have a hard time saying I'm disabled or admitting it unless I'm joking or want someone to feel sorry for me. My coping mechanisms include me making fun of myself, so I can beat anyone to the punch of pointing out the obvious. I am always the girl in the room that only looks like nothing is wrong with me until I start shaking uncontrollably, and my body throws me forward. Then I am super conscious of the people sneaking stares to see what is going on with me or my favorite; are you having a seizure, ma'am? Are you okay? This usually ends in me assuring the Individual that I am okay, and this is just part of my everyday life. These days I can't tell if I am guilty of pimping my own illness or if this is just what I tell myself to feel like I am still in control. Apart from me knowing that I am guilty of manipulation here and there, I justify my actions because, in hindsight, that is the only good thing about this illness, along with the VIP parking, Walmart scooters, and folks that just allow me to jump any line if I begin to exhibit an episode. (and no, I have never faked an episode).

People have an interesting way of treating the disabled, either they are extremely nice and compassionate to you or just simply rude. I have never experienced in-between.

How has this affected me? I miss my loft a lot of times and the endless sunshine that it is providing from the countless windows wrapping the apartment. I miss going skating and attending open mics. I now have to consider if venues are handicap accessible or friendly. I know it may be selfish of me, but honestly, if my disability hit today, I would book a ticket to a place with sun and a beach then turn off my phone for five days. It's hard going through the wintertime with severe depression and not being able to go out unless someone drives you. I apologize if this section sounds like a boring rant now. I guess I honestly just needed to purge during this section and share my innermost thoughts. I am tired of crying and feeling sorry for myself, though, as I type, by now, you get the point Syringomyelia sucks!! Never take your health and strength for granted. God had to use a rare illness to humble me in some areas and get my attention, but at the end of the day, I wouldn't wish this on my worst enemy. My experience of living with this illness is really for God's glory, and He will heal me in his expected time only. I know I won't be like this for the next ten years; sometimes, I just have to remind myself.

GOD USES ANYTHING
FOR HIS GLORY

On the evening of Feb. 17[th.] I assumed it would be like any other personal care day I take. You know, just the typical go find a booth, some amazing comfort food, and just be to myself, well at least that was the plan. However, God had other plans for me, and those included unconventional ministry His way. As if my whole illness wasn't ministry too. "Hey, remember You told me this all would be for your glory. I didn't sign up for being Mother Theresa!" (me yelling to Jesus on the days I have to cope with depression).

One day, I wasn't quite sure where I was going to eat, so I allowed my stomach to lead me, at least I thought. The Holy Spirit and Google's menu led me to 3 Kings. I was blessed to take an Uber there and back because two of the saints blessed me with cab fare. As I arrived at the venue that particular night, the place was almost dead customer wise. There were maybe six other couples in the restaurant, including me. I opted out of sitting in the front and decided to choose a cozy booth in the back of the restaurant. This portion of 3 Kings was dimly lit, quiet, with no other human in sight besides the waiters going back and forth into the kitchen. Three kings, a cute little pub, was the perfect balance of bar meets high-end restaurant! With exposed red brick, hardwood floors all the way throughout the entire venue, and a raised sitting area, that makes you feel separated from the rest, kind of like VIP, but still a part of the room.

I seated myself, and a waiter approached me instantly to greet me with the menu. Man, I tell you good customer service is hard to come by, but this person made and initial awesome 1st impression on me. I mean, don't you hate those establishments you enter in whether they be bars or even a five scale place that fail to acknowledge you once you enter the place. Oh, and my favorite, you have to constantly hunt down your waiter to the point that it takes away from your entire experience. Well, as I overlooked the menu, all I could think was I was so glad I listened to that inner voice to stop here. This was exactly what I needed. Also, why do I always end up at the most romantic places alone, but that's neither here nor there. You see, I had already done my homework prior to coming to the establishment, so I pretty much knew what I wanted. Yes, I am one of those people, picky, and planner. My go-to rule when visiting a new eatery is to go with what they are known for. So, I went with something as simple as wings, because surely one couldn't go wrong there, or at least I thought.

As I start adding up how much this peace of mind will cost me, I noticed I didn't bring my money. Can you imagine the look of panic on my face as I realized after ordering that I had no cash? Well, I will tell you that my survival instincts kicked in, and I thought about faking a seizure since people always think I'm having one anyway. I know I know that so wrong of me, but seriously I was a black woman in this mainly white establishment. I had heard about in movies of how they make you wash dishes, but I knew my black butt would go to jail.

After much consideration and panicking, I thought to myself someone has to love me enough to help a sister out because I did, in fact, have the money it was just at home. So, I set my pride aside and hit up everyone in my instant message I could think of. While I was thinking of a master plan, the waiter kept coming by asking how my meal was and everything. Listen, I couldn't even think straight, let alone did I want to be bothered with excessive niceness in an attempt to get a good tip at this moment. Cause truth be told, if I didn't come up on some money, we both would be screwed. So, I ate slowly for the 1st time in my life, trying to stall the time.

Finally, poet Knowledge blessed me along with Brittany and two other people. At this point, I had more than enough for my meal, tip, and a little extra. Whew. Thank you, Jesus was all I could think. Now that I was able to enjoy my meal is when things took another interesting turn. I happened to notice this waitress that kept going back and forth from the kitchen to the dining area. She would occasionally wipe her face to get rid of the evidence that she was totally losing it at that moment. I don't know why, but I zoomed in on her. I had seen that look before, the one where you are experiencing a crisis and trying to keep it together because you're in public.

Finally, after staring at her for about 10 minutes, the Holy Spirit encouraged me to ask what was wrong. This lady began to spill her guts to me about how her brother had just overdosed on heroin and died. I told her I knew about that all too well as I too had overdosed just a month ago and almost died. She said, wow, how long had I been sober now. I chuckled and told her my testimony about Syringomyelia and almost dying from antidepressants.

After she heard my story, she was shocked to hear I had been through so much and to be so young. She apologized for venting to me, a complete stranger, and for ruining my dinner. I told her that It was completely fine, and I even offered to give her a hug. Afterward, she walked off to attend to her other tables as I am preparing to check out the Spirit prompts me to pray for the young lady. I laughed and said to myself, if you wanted me to do ministry Jesus, you didn't have to give me a scare like that. I would have just did it! So I signaled for the waitress again and asked if I could pray for her. Excited and surprised at the same time, she assures me that it's perfectly fine and even mentions that she has been trying to pray for months. After I prayed, Casey, the waitress, sits down and chats with me some more. She continues to apologize for ranting to me about her issues, but I assured her that it didn't bother me. It seemed like she really did need a listening ear, and apparently, this is what God had sent me there for.

To lighten up the mood, I told her about how I almost contemplated faking a seizure to pay my bill. Shocked, she made mention of why I didn't just ask her for help with it. Her gesture left me in even more shock as well, that a stranger would go to such lengths to help me when they owe me nothing. Casey asked if she could give me her number and joked how I didn't have to use the number if I didn't want to. I assured her that I'm a woman of my word, and I would give her a courtesy call to check in with her. Casey kept calling me an angel of some sort and asked if she could walk me to the door.

It's funny to me because this stranger, in such a short period of time, felt indebted to me but little did she know I owed Jesus, the Man who prompted me to do everything. I forgot to mention after my heart stopped racing, and my mind cancels out all the ways of getting out of washing dishes. I managed to call my God mom and share with her the funny story of almost going to jail. She laughed so hard and long on the phone and said I made her night.

Now, although I didn't find it to be funny at all because I was living it, she reminded me that I was a total character, and it wasn't the act itself that was funny but how I told the story. Later we both agreed since she got to laugh at my pain, she should pay for my dessert. She Cashapp me $5, and I headed over to Insomnia for my dessert. I got two scoops of ice cream with just enough chocolate that the worker had scraped from the bottom of the barrel for me. Talking a whole night full of just favor for little old me. I took an Uber back home and shook my head in disbelief that my life is always some book yet to be written or movie. Because surely people don't experience these silly supernatural occurrences that I am having with a hint of comedy.

DM CHRONICLES

By now, you're probably thinking to yourself, Nicole, why air out all your business? I mean, somethings should be kept to yourself, right? However, I think for way too long as Christians, we have prescribed to only sharing the testimonies that make us look good. I know that's not the case when it comes to you bishop, minister, and pastor so and so. However, many saints really do this. I also believe it is because of this philosophy we have adopted that so many others are not set free and delivered. We have to be willing to tell the good, bad, and even the ugly because just maybe there is a youth sitting in the pew ready to walk away from the faith because of this preconceived notion that the church has taught them that everyone is perfect. And if you are not well, your faith is not strong enough or my favorite, you just don't love God enough. Well, let me help someone in this portion of the book. Many of your favorite preachers, God covered them in the midst of their mess and still greatly uses them! They may be operating in the midst of rebellion right now, but gifts come without repentance and God can use whoever He wants whenever He chooses to in order to get His message through. There were so many times I messed up big time in private, and nobody knew. I often think about what if all my ugly skeletons were blasted like some of these mega preachers. Would some still considering me to be God's woman or not?Shoot, would they still feel like I can get a prayer through?

Maybe it's my flesh or immaturity, but I have been pulled aside a few times about the things I post on social media, and rather it's appropriate or not for me to say as a minister. Apart from when I feel convicted, I will go back and delete some people because the spirit deals with me, while other parts feel the public needs to see some of these outbursts too. I'm not perfect, and everything that comes out my mouth is not politically correct or church etiquette. Hey, I can admit the fact that my ministry is not for everyone. I also understand and thank God I'm not a Bishop or Pastor. I'm just a little too sarcastic and still immature for that role, which leads me to my DM chronicles.

No one ever wishes to talk about the elephant in the room when it comes to singles walking in Christianity. We mumble about it in private but scratch the surface at single conferences, but still, no one wants to keep it real. So, I guess I will... I will be willing to say what I wish some youth pastors and other leaders would be so bold to say.

I am a Christian single that struggles with being lonely often to the point that it's pitiful, and I have compromised my integrity. I also deal with being horry often, and I beat up on myself so much as if I expect these organs not to work anymore until some Boaz finds whatever man we model our husband be like in the bible. It does not matter how many gospel songs I meditate on or what amazing fast I come off of. Still, I am reminded that this flesh of mine still exists.

In the middle of the night well around 8 and 9, that is, I have my favorite people that I love to DM. You know those old flames that probably should have been mentioned in my chapter about men. I have my faithful two this week that I know I can count on; see with these men, I'm not a minister or the perfect Nicole I pretend to be on my page. To be honest, that good girl persona turns them on even more, so, we play this cat and mouse game, but it always has to be by my rules. If they engage too quickly, and the conversation goes way left, I quickly remind them who I am. As if it's my saving grace or badge of honor or something. Like, don't you see these quotes, scriptures, and prayer requests written all over my page, sir. If the screenshot got a glimpse of some of your advances towards me, I wouldn't be able to explain myself out of this one. So I always keep the conversation at a level 6 of heathen.

Because all I really want is to be flirted with, receive sweet advances, reminded how beautiful I am, and by all means, stroke my ego just a tad bit so I can play dumb about this game we play once a week. But remember the rules, I don't do d*ck pics or insinuations about sex and positions. Your mind can imagine me because I don't want my DM guy to know about my messed-up struggles to stay pure. I don't want to insinuate I've never had consensual sex before. So we do this tap dance with our flirting back and forth until I'm bored or either convicted. Then, that is when my analytical mind begins to rationalize with my behavior, and I hit myself with the whole God is not through with me yet. I mean, I'm not doing anything wrong. But I know that one day I am going to take that flirt way too far, and the enemy, in his own clever way, will get me to compromise my integrity in writing.

Shoot, just about a week ago, one of my DM favorites, in his own witty and flirty way, took it too far. I felt dirty afterward and asked myself, why dc I continue to put myself through these empty conversations that only feed my flesh. These men are only space fillers, we definitely are not equally yoked, and they are nothing more than something good for the eyes to look at. To me, t's just a reminder that I still got it and can pull something fine and desirable from the world's point of view. But where does that leave me when my bearded favorite not once but three insist on sharing with me how he wants to eat my cookies anc suck on something that should be meant for my husband's eyes only. I apologize if this is too vulgar for some, but I'm trying to keep it as real and tasteful as possible.

Singles, Satan is crafty, and even when it comes to the strongest of us. He knows I would never willingly jump into a conversation that starts off with a request to taste and suck on me or entertain them. However, he knows I will go for the ones that compliment how beautiful I am and make comments about how they wish they could hold me at that moment. Because those conversations, if entertained long enough, leads to comments about booty rubs and everything else we deem permissible by all the times, we keep silent when they push it too far in the conversation. This is my struggle; I'm a hopeless romantic that loves compliments, and sometimes I'm horny as hell! God is not concerned with my obsession with romanticism, but he is concerned with how It plays out in His daughter's life. He is concerned with the open doors it allows for the enemy to run rapid in my life.

Lastly, He is concerned about how it later shows up in my character. If I think these harmful flirts in the midnight hour are having no impact on me, then I'm lying to myself. What you feed your spirit, it becomes the spirit of rejection, and what it breeds is real.

BROKENNESS

HAS NO GENDER

I remember the first time I heard Jackie Hill-Perry's poem on YouTube "My life as a Stud." The year had to be around 2009 or 2010. For the 1st time, someone wrote in a poem what years I had been trying to articulate in not so many words. I even remember the day I inboxed her on Fb. This was way before she became a household name. However, even then, I wasn't quite ready to wrestle with the demons that had held me hostage, for years. You see, my best friend is a HUGE advocate for the LGBTQ community, and she literally is like one of my favorite people. Though what I am about to share in this chapter, some will label me a hypocrite, homophobic, and everything else under the sun, but this is my truth. If you don't like it or agree with it, shoot write your own book and use that as your own pulpit to share your opinions. I never did quite know how to put into words my inner thoughts about the topic because my relationship with it is all too complicated.

So here it goes, my first interaction with the same sex had to be around age 6 or 7. I only know that I was school age, but still able to go to daycare. I was spending the night at the daycare owners' house, Ela, along with her two nieces. One name Victoria who was my childhood best friend. We played the night away like any other typical sleepover. Then someone suggested we play house, except in our scenario, no one was the correct gender to play the daddy. So, if I remember correctly, I offered to be the daddy.

In our innocence, we portrayed what we had seen in our own homes and on tv. We told Victoria to go to her room since she was the child, then the other young lady and I pretended to go to sleep since we were the mom and dad as we laid under an infant's crib because of her aunt's home had been converted to a daycare. The young lady and I started making out as if we were a real mommy and daddy. Despite our innocence in the act at such a young age, conviction began to become activated in me, and I stopped it. That was my first encounter as a child with the same sex. That moment would create a vicious cycle of shame, guilt, curiosity, and confusion for the rest of my entire life. As I got older and went off into high school, words such as gay, lesbian, and stud were thrown around so loosely. Way before I could understand or even articulate what pleasure two women could gain from one another. In high school, I was socially awkward, and it felt like everyone was having sex and talking about it except me. Shoot, my first sex education talks came from the girls' locker room and the girl who bragged about their sexuality and wore it with a badge. These conversations ranged from their 1st time they had sex and how bad it hurt to the dos and don'ts about oral sex

What many don't know, it was because of those locker room conversations that I stayed a virgin so long. A girl could only take so many conversations about STDs and how bad it hurts when the guy tries to break your hymen. Right then and there, I decided I was good on sex because, let's be honest, my pain tolerance sucked. During my early 20's with those I allowed to get to 1st base, they all had a nickname for me. They used to call me "blue balls" I would tease a guy so bad and only allow him to explore above the waist that to the point he got blue balls. I found this nickname to be some badge of honor and a form of power for me.

No one needed to know I was afraid of sex, and this way, I could still get my issue off too, which leads me into how I fell into liking girls. It was never so much that I desired to sleep with women because that didn't come until many years later. I just loved the sensual ways of a woman. I loved how they were less scary then men, and they flirted ten times better too. With women like men, they also fed my ego, but it was never pressured about sex, at least I thought.

The first woman I ever tried to kiss had a history of turning girls like me out, heterosexuals. She was a tomboy, super laid back, and identified herself as a stud. This young lady and I, later on, became friends, and to protect her identity, we will just call her the Photographer. Well, the Photographer graduated U. City a few years earlier than me and worked across the street from my job. It's funny in school, I never spoke to the girl, but we became close friends through FB, I think. I would end my 8 hr. shift every night and then go to her job and sit another 5 hours or so with her. She was intriguing to me and rough around the edges in a good way. She was the 1st person to ever get me to go to a club. Then, later on, a gay club; I will revisit that in a little second. I promise it's a funny store.

During that summer, Photographer and I became super close! To the point that I use to look forward to our hangouts at the gas station. She legit was my friend, and despite my corniness, she got me.

Well, she invited me out to a club one night that turned out to be a gay club called 'Attitudes". Now let me just say I was way in over my head with this one. I had no experience with clubs, let alone a gay club. She gave me all the rules on how to have a good time. I was enccuraged not to make eye contact with other women for a long period. This was code for I was interested and never be too friendly; this, of course, is a gay club. The night was going well until I broke one of those rules. After slightly tipsy, I made eye contact accidentally with a stud across the room that decided to shoot her shot. She gave me all her best lines and asked me to dance. Thankfully my friend showed up and told her we were together. This was, of course, after scolding me for breaking the rules. I must have been a magnet for the aggressive type in the club because right after she left me again, someone approached me a second time, but it was a trans.

Now, this is where the story gets sketchy; all I remember was being cornered by a tall man or woman who was 10 sec away from taking my cookies in that club. I was so scared, but my friend came to my rescue and told the individual we were together. Stuttering, I just kept agreeing with her and whatever would get me out of the corner with this aggressive person ready to stick their teeth in me. For the sake of time, I will get to my whole point about telling this particular story. Well, as the night wrapped up, my friend dropped me off at my crib. That night I don't know if it was the liquor or my courage talking, possibly both. After about 20 minutes ago, I yelled across the street while leaving the club that this one girl had a fat ass. So, I decided to ask my homegirl about how she turns girls out because my curiosity was killing me, and she told me all these juicy stories, and then I mustered up the courage to ask her if she could kiss me.

See, I had never kissed a girl before that whole daycare incident. She immediately refused to, but after some clever begging, I convinced her. I can't remember what ignorant comment I made after that, but she ended up kicking me out of her car, and let's just say I never got that kiss. Which looking back on it now, I am glad. To this day, I still consider her a friend and the beginning stages of how we met, and that particular night we never really discuss.

My curiosity about women continued to grow. I should have left it as thoughts because I kept poking a bear that eventually would wake up, and I would have to pray and fast to put it back down. My other childhood friend, Dreads, when we were 17/18, identified herself as bisexual. In my 1st couple of years of curiosity, she would be my google for all questions. I remember being 17 ard spending the night at her house. Her sister came into the room to ask her something. Little did she know she had caught me in a very uncomfortable position. At that very moment, ol girl literally had her hand comfortably placed on my vagina, attempting to do God knows what. I don't even know how we got to that point. My friend was way freer in her sexuality than I was, and quite frankly, I never stopped her attempts that day under the cover. Now, she never did go all the way, but she did fondle me for what felt like several minutes under those covers. This again was the 1st time I felt shame behind the act when her baby sister walked in on us.

By the time I was in my early 20's, I was still not quite certain what two women do with each other because up until this point, I had only been kissed and fondle. However, my inner actions with Wordsmith would forever change this. You see, Wordsmith was older than me. I was mesmerized by this person; not only was she slick with words, but she was my favorite person to flirt with. We would talk on the phone and flirt all the time. Well, she eventually got tired of our phone interactions and invited me to lunch one day.

I can remember exactly what I was wearing. I had my favorite dark denim jeans and a fitted white tee shirt. We were supposed to go to Goody Goody because I had never been there before, but the line was super crazy. So we ended up at Bread Co in the loop, which was perfect. I ordered watermelon, juice, and a blueberry muffin. We chatted and laughed, and what I felt was harmless would, later on, take a crazy turn where I would have to put my money where my mouth was. After she dropped me off at home, she presented me with a gift, a teddy bear, a card, and some candy sugar babies.

Now, you would have to know our interaction to understand the symbolics behind these sweet gestures. Well, as I thanked her for the gifts, she began to make a few advances towards me and ended up inside my home. I remember making a thousand excuses on why she couldn't come up, but she was determined. She asked where everyone was, and I told her my granny was gone, and my grandfather was outside cutting the grass. What happened after that, I don't quite remember, step by step, but I do remember taking a small wash up and entering back into my bedroom. I also remember sitting awkwardly on the edge of my bed.

I wasn't ready to take that step with someone, but yet I obliged her request. Even with my pants down, I still didn't want to do it, but it happened anyway. I never enjoyed the act, but I will never forget the comment she made afterward to me, she said I tasted like teddy grams or something like that.

I guess that was supposed to be a compliment or something and then she asked to go again. Afterward, I felt dirty, confused, and wishing I could talk to someone who wouldn't judge me.

To this day, I have never been able to have that HARD conversation with Wordsmith about what went down that day. A part of me felt like I played just as much as a part as she did. I mean, you just can't be flirting with grown folks for weeks and making empty promises you don't plan to cash. Shoot, I guess I just underestimated how much she was really about that life. I enjoyed the harmless flirting, but I never liked a woman enough to engage in that part.

The woman, later on, became one of my FAVORITE people in life... period. We never crossed that line in our friendship again, and later on, she mentioned to me that it should have never gotten that far, to begin with. I guess that statement within itself gave me some kind of healing. I won't be completely healed until I can look at that person in the face and ask them why it couldn't just stop at lunch. I felt violated in a way and have looked at them differently ever since.

Now, by all means, I am not trying to play the victim here. To this day, I would give this person a kidney if they ever needed one, facts! I am simply just speaking on the truth that later on bloomed to an awesome friendship. Some people may say, Nicole, that's just way too complicated for me. And to that person, I would respond, screw you. When I almost died after my suicide, that same individual visited me in the hospital and has given me a shoulder to cry on many days during the depression. A few people could learn a lesson or two about genuine kindness from her! In a nutshell, keep your mouth off my Wordsmith. I am very overprotective of my friends.

This next person I engaged with, I met while living in a homeless shelter in Vegas. She was wild, young, and out of control. Pieces of me told myself I could save her, so I befriended her. Right off the back, she showed interest in me and would constantly make advances towards me. Despite the fact, I turned every advance down, she never stopped. I would sometimes even give her my debit card to buy food and small items. Smh, I was just nice like that. Well, in this particular shelter, the girls all lived on one side of the building and the guys on the other side. Girls were never allowed in the guys' room and vice versa, only in the common areas. This never stopped Mel, though. She marched to the beat of her own drum haven't been raised by the streets mainly. She often used men for money and whatever else she wanted. She would boast about her ability to manipulate men so well and get what she wanted. These guys would literally come to the shelter and drop her off clothes and money, I can't make this up. The sight of this was trippy within itself. I guess she was manipulating me too because every time she asked for my card, I gave it to her. People in the shelter would even ask me why I would always give her my card. I would just insist I was a nice person and to mind your business.

One night it was rainy, and I was missing home like crazy and horny on top of that. I thought it was wise to vent to Mel about my issues. She advised me she could help me with that problem of mine. This child really did have a huge ego because she even talked like a man when she was hitting on you. That always confused me, like I wanted to remind her of the fact that she did not know she was a whole woman. That night she kept asking me over and over did I want her to take care of that for me. Even went on to say, "I can make you feel good." I eventually gave in and said, sure. As quickly as I said yes, she was at my door before I could change my mind and talk her out of it. Even while she was in my room, I kept trying to talk her out of it. Well, that never worked because I ended up on the bathroom sink in an uncomfortable position; she obliviously had done this one before. After complaining, I wasn't comfortable; I ended up by the tub. The night ended in moans and more confusion. Every time I got into it; conviction hit like a pile of bricks being thrown back at me. I will never admit it to her because her ego is already too big, but that was the BEST oral sex I have ever had, and I've only done it three other times.

Look, I am not trying to turn this book into some cheesy version of a Zane book by all means. It is my intention to give the truth in a way that doesn't portray me to be all so perfect. The next day I woke up feeling like crap and a person that had way too many drinks and made several bad decisions. Again I felt guilt, shame, and emptiness. Why did I keep doing this to myself? This time I justified my actions with at least I enjoyed it, and it took the edge off me. I mean, I could repent later, right?? However, the Holy Ghost had other plans for me. See, I had just been baptized in Jesus' Name only a month ago. And while some Christians may have you to believe after baptism, you are as white as snow and won't sin again, that is so not the case. In fact, I barely made it past 30 days before I would spit in God's face to satisfy my fleshy needs. So, I did what I had been taught my whole life. I called up my 1st Lady, and I confessed all my dirty little sins.

No, I am not Catholic, but that phone confession changed the trajectory of my entire life! My 1st Lady prayed with me and asked me if I really wanted to be delivered. I told her I was tired of being like this; I needed Jesus to help! She prayed for me, and I repented from my belly as my face was covered in tears. I thank her for not judging me and being so cool about it. That was the 1st time in my life I admit to another Christian or even confessed what I struggled with.

Well, years went by, and I didn't have any slip-ups. Until 2019 of last year. I met another person who we will just call Black n Mild. I met Black n Mild at the grocery store across the street from my loft. She was loud, blunt, wild with a beautiful set of teeth to match and attitude that lived with no regrets. We were what you would call polar opposites. Here I go again thinking I could save people.You would think I would have learned my lesson by now with Mel. I guess that is why this book is called, "I love Jesus, but need THERAPY." Such an appropriate title for such a jacked up and complex person such as myself.

Yes, I should have run to the hills after my 1st hangout with Black n Mild that night after her shift. See my slow, no friend having self-thought it was a good idea to go get drinks and get to know this person. She insisted we meet at this restaurant across the street from her job. So that night, I paid for an overly priced milkshake that wasn't even good and saw every sign I needed to know why I should run to the hills. Black n Mild could throw her liquor back, and although I was the idiot who suggested a drink when I didn't drink. I have to admit I found her company to be quite amusing to me. That summer, every day I would enter the Culinary, we would address each other as besties with a goofy high-five to follow. It started off as a joke to insult her friendliness, and what can I say, the chick just ran w th it.

Over the months, I learned Black n Mild had a story to tell too. She came from a successful family of business owners, and although every day was a hot girl summer for her. There was so much untapped potential in her that I always wished she had cultivated. She bragged how she used men for money, and her favorite slogan when I asked what she planned to get into was always," Baldheaded hoe stuff, of course, friend."

Black n Mild always made sure I ate and was never hungry, and she had a big heart! I just resented how much she was an alcoholic and placed herself in dangerous situations. One day when I asked to have a girls' night out with her at her house, she said yes. As usual, she pregamed with Henny and too many blunts too count. I mean this child count put some liquor back. I don't know what was going on with me, but one minute I was chilling in the bed watching Netflix with my friend. Then the next morning, I entertained the unthinkable. Placing kisses strategically on her chest, I joked about how 6 minutes was more than enough time to spare before work. I don't know if my imagination had got the best of me or way too many movies, but I actually was going to do this. Like, I was having conversations with myself in the middle of committing to the act. Finally, as my head discovered her peach, I guess the prayers of my mother, Godmother, had finally reached me because I snapped so hard out of it! Like a sober drunk, I couldn't imagine how I got there.

Ashamed and embarrassed as she too was sobering up and still fully clothed, I came up from under the covers. I called my Uber again for work and never mumbled a word about that morning. I just kept thanking Jesus for creating a scapegoat and allowing me not to go there.

Like, seriously, I wouldn't have even known what to do, or where to begin with. Everything is not like the movies Nicole, and you are way too blunt for that kind of interaction, not to mention the soul ties that follow it. Afterward, I always hated when people insinuated at her job that I might be gay. It was as if they could see right through me even though they couldn't quite put their finger on what it was about me. I hung out with Black n Mild several times after that, but it was never like that. I had one job to do, and that was interceding for her. Yes, you just heard me correctly; the same person that entertained eating this person out, God had mandated me to pray for her soul.

Over the course of those months, I prayed and ministered to her. I thank God for protecting my witness and allowing me to keep clean hands because the enemy knew if I had gone down that morning, it would have impacted my witness and my ability to minister to this person. See, despite her bluntness, she had a reverence and respect for what I stood for. For a person that didn't do church, she allowed me to share about Jesus and even pray for her. I could tell God was doing some kind of work in her and chipping away at some things in her life.

The last night I spent at Black n Mild's house was a Godly intervention. She left me to make a weed run and didn't come back until like 2 am in the morning. Well, Jesus had it to go down like that because the moment she left, the spirit came over me, and I began to pace the floor under the unction of the Holy Ghost and pray one of the most powerful prayers I have ever prayed. I prayed so long I'm sure I lost weight and sweated out my outfit. I prayed until I lost my voice. I prayed so hard. The spirit just kept having me say her name and repeat come forth, come forth in the Name of Jesus! I binded up every spirit I could think of and anointed her entire house and shoes. Once I got done praying, it was either midnight or 1 am and still no sign of her, and out of anger and concern, I took a short nap. After I woke from my nap, I was concerned that something could have happened to her, so I prayed and asked God to bring her home safely within the next 15 minutes. As I went to close my eyes the 2nd time, she came up the stairs drunk and high as hell.

That was the last night I spent the night at her house. I tried to hang out several times after that, but it never happened. God severed the friendship before she started having more of an impact on me than I have on her. To this day, I still have love for her and know God simply allowed me to sow a seed. Besides, scripture says one sow, one water, but it is God that giveth the increase. (1 Corinthians 3:6-9).

By now, I know you are thinking well I definitely didn't expect that type of outcome, and neither did I. I guess a part of me saw Black n Mild like a little sister that I felt I needed to protect from the world. I always found myself calling to check up on her after every shift. I always feared she would buy weed from the wrong janky weed man or get drunk with the wrong crowd. Rape culture is real, and everyone is not so free-spirited as she is.

That child gave me so many headaches and caused me to lose so many hours of sleep praying for her safety and protection, but I guess every thank you was payment enough. That and the fact she mentioned she didn't really have real friends that truly cared about her. In this way, I told myself I was doing God's work. I made it my goal to show her people can care and not want anything in return from her.

She always made fun of me from my naive ways and the ability to see the good in people. While I felt sorry for her careless and dangerous approach towards life. I mean jumping in Ubers when you're so drunk you can't remember your own address while still managing to find your way to my house; oh, you better know she got a nice motherly scold out of me. I also thanked the Uber driver for watching out for my friend. He told her that she was lucky to have someone like me. My prayer for Black n Mild is that she is healed from her trauma as I am currently working on mine as I write this book. I only want what's best for and for her to succeed.

Despite that crazy morning and whatever crazy spirit that was, that came over me. I know some people may not believe in possession, but I felt like I was possessed because when I came to, I realized those actions were not me. Despite my history with women, I meant it when I told God I was done with that lifestyle. I am not sure if I was being completely honest with the reader if I am all the way delivered because I still struggle with always looking at women's butts no matter where I am. It's like my alter ego has a thing for butts and the plump kind. It doesn't care if I'm in church or at the grocery store. I stay complimenting women's butt in my mind. I said all this to say and went this elaborate maze to tell my personal story because I know I'm not the only one. I always knew homosexuality was a sin, and Jesus didn't approve of it.

To this day, you cannot convince me that it is not a spirit like anything else except that it is rooted in rejection, sin, perversion, and sexual trauma. I believe that door was opened in my childhood that night at the slumber party, and my actions and curiosity simply just continued to feed the spirit. However, I am a witness that my mother's prayers kept and covered me to the point a part of me was always trying to fight my flesh. That's why I could never completely enjoy the sin without separating myself from God. I do not prescribe to the belief we are born gay, but we are born and shaped into iniquity and sin!! I hate how Christians have ignored every other sin under the sun and magnified homosexuality. God hates ALL sin, including adultery, blasphemy, drunkenness, liars, and those who bear false witness. We cannot make an impact with the gay community until we address the fact that SIN is SIN and quit picking the ones we choose to acknowledge.

Also, love and consistency have won more battles than judgment. My 1st lady was able to minister to me that morning in Vegas because she first established a relationship with me. Then she, later on, held me accountable when I confessed my sins. It was her love that allowed me to receive her open rebuke. It was also that same love that caused me to want to do and be better.

Now, while God would not have us to shack up with sin and become buddy-buddy. A wise person once told me no one cares what you know until they know how much you care. Black n Mild was only able to receive my prayers despite my shortcomings because I was consistent, and I didn't beat her with judgment. Now, did I hold her accountable, yes?

However, I listened to the leading and guiding of the Holy Spirit on the right times to witness and how to witness. There are many people who I love dearly and would give a whole organ that identifies as being gay or bi. However, I continue to pray for their full deliverance in Jesus' Name.

Wow, realizing I have to create healthy boundaries myself. I can't flirt with sin and justify my actions just because I'm not committing the act itself. I will be the first to call myself the biggest hypocrite there is. I understand that by my inability to address my own issues of rejection and love, it opened the door for the enemy to try me in that area of my life. However, my soul loves Jesus, and without excusing my sin, I continue to press toward the mark. I want to please God with every bone in my body because my YES is for real! I don't feel like I could have ever had a for-real blown-out relationship with a woman because, to be honest, I just wasn't about that life. There was no way you convince me to go down on a woman. Now, a free meal or flirting here or there I would willingly sign up for.

Though regardless, God was not pleased with any of my games and excuses. Just because I longed for attention, it didn't mean that I should allow the enemy to attach a stronghold to me that would take over a decade to be delivered from. Any time we play with sin, regardless if we find it to be harmless in our own reasoning or not, we will always lose! The devil will always get us to push the envelope so far to a place that we can't come back from. Where only Jesus himself can pick up the species. I fought LONG and HARD about sharing this last chapter in my book. It is some who will call them my dirtiest of secrets, which I never did a good job of keeping a secret.

Many have whispered and even insinuated that I was gay. Whatever title you wish to place on me is neither here nor there. I will say this is God's eyes, I was summed up in one word, a SINNER that needed to be saved. I am shaking in my boots of what folks will think of me after writing this book. However, a part of me was healed, delivered, and even set free after writing this. I may have had to stop several times in tears and with disgust as I took a hard look at myself. See, we may be able to hide from people, but we can never hide from the God of the universe. He knows us better than anyone does. I know now Jesus needed me to write this section so the enemy could no longer have anything to hang over my head when he finally does elevate me in ministry. There won't be any tell-all books with my name included or a news headline because I have already told it all in GREAT detail.

This is why I felt the need to be as detailed as possible. The Lord told me two years ago through the writing of this book, women would be saved and come forth and tell me their story because of my own transparency. Yes, the journey was HARD, and Satan tried to convince me to leave parts out that didn't show me in the best way. However, my desire is to please God above anything else. For he said in his word that he is magnified through our very weaknesses. For what is impossible for men are possible for God; I want to encourage someone today. I serve God, where nothing is too hard for him! He takes the LEAST of us and uses us for his glory.

It is my prayer that this book will save millions of souls. I decree and declare that there will be an outpour of testimonies birthed from this writing! I declare that those identifying as gay or lesbian will be set free! I declare those who suffer from childhood trauma will receive the healing that they need to move on in Jesus' Name.I declare that women will be healed completely from all sexual trauma prior to marriage. I declare that ministers, pastors, and bishops would begin to have a posture of true repentance because one servant was bold enough to tell the whole truth no matter how ugly and bad it made her look. Jesus is real! He is waiting to save, deliver, and set you free, the reader of this book.

Yes, I did cry a river and almost died last year from starting what the enemy knew would bless thousands. My process and complete deliverance may not be fully done, but I am allowing God to do the work in every area that concerns me. Give God a try, what else do you have to lose? I know without fail, ALL the things people love about me is because of Jesus, and without Him, I am nothing!!! I love Jesus, but I truly do need Therapy, and that's alright because I am in the hands of Him while on the potters' wheel. "Being confident of this very thing, that He which has begun a good work in (me) will perform it until the day of Jesus Christ"! Philippians 1:6

God is not through with me yet. I take confidence in the fact that before I was formed, he knew me in my mother's womb; before I was born, he set me apart and appointed me as a prophet to the nations. Jesus is not looking for perfect people. He is, however, looking for imperfect people to perform his PERFECT Will through. Amen!

I want to take the time to thank you, the reader, for reading my story, the good, the bad, and the ugly. Hopefully, I made you laugh, think, and really to take into consideration your walk with God. By all means, I am not the poster child for Christianity, as you can see if you made it to the end of this book... lol. Yet, with everything I have done and seen, I am still convinced Jesus is real. I also know if I had to do life over again, while I would do several things differently, accepting Christ into my life would not change.

I tell my mother all the time; the best thing she could have ever given me was Jesus and teaching me how to pray.

Those two things had sustained and kept me when I didn't want to be kept. And even when the enemy had plans to take me out indefinite, it was God's saving grace that said, not today you can't have this one because I have work for her to do. Jesus doesn't need you to be perfect before you give your life to Him. He does, however, need you to realize just how bad you really do need Him. Don't allow church hurt to keep you from God or toxic Christians working out their own trauma that they didn't realize they were hurting you in the process. Unforgiveness, when left undealt with breeds into bitterness, and bitterness can literally kill you. Learn from my stupid mistakes.

We all can agree we love Jesus, but there is NOTHING wrong with partnering him with therapy too. I see my therapist faithfully every week. I want to be whole within myself so that God can use me as he sees fit. Take those meds and create boundaries with your loved ones. Don't allow anyone to tell you that you love God any less because you have to take medication. Jesus gave us medicine and doctors for a reason. Okay, so I don't have anything else to write now. I just wanted to really drive home the point that we can love Jesus but still need therapy too.

MY CONCLUSION

AND THEN THERE WAS ONE

Imagine almost losing your life, and then Jesus tells you that your diagnosis with Syringomyelia is all for His glory. So, you cope with the illness, only for Him to come back and tell you one more thing... Nicole, I need you to let go of every person you ever called friend/family for the last 15 years. Now, if being diagnosed with a handicap didn't rock my world, this prophecy certainly did. The Lord told me there were eight people in my life, friends to be exact, that I needed to let go. These people didn't pour into me spiritually, nor did they respect the God I serve and some of what I stood for. As my analytical mind raced through names imaging who that could be. I took out a piece of paper and began to write down all those who were the closest to me and those I called a friend.

My heart broke as I thought about the possibility that these people had to be cut out of my life. I pleaded with God for weeks over some and even played dumb with the last 3. Like you really want me to let go of my best friend, Jesus. I am already a loner by nature. My favorite, Lightskin has seen me through every homeless situation and mental breakdown I could think of. She even tried to go to every doctor's visit with me, but I didn't let her. So the 1st person I cut out of my life was hard, and they even called me a hypocrite and a few other religious slanders. That breakup broke me, but quite frankly, the friendship had been over, and I was tired of my efforts not being reciprocated on her end, so I felt relieved in a sense.

The next breakup was emotional for me. I cried before I got the courage to tell the person I couldn't be friends with them. I told her our relationship had come towards an end and reassured that it was nothing personal. Lord knows I lied through my teeth. I never told her that just a few days prior, God gave me a strong rebuke concerning her and even called her a witch in the spirit. All I could ever see after that on her profile pic was demons and what she was engaging with. This always stayed as a reminder for what I kept putting off. I loved this person dearly by how they saw me through their eyes. I shared things with her that no one knew, and a part of me felt indebted to her because the night I committed suicide, she single-handedly, along with my BFF, put out an amber alert for my black butt. That alone spoke volumes to me on just how much she loved me. She always cared about my mental health and helped me get through rough financial times. She doesn't know this, but I plan to bless her in a huge financial way for every cash app she gave when I needed it the most, and she was struggling too. I wish you well if you have stumbled across my book and read this section. I apologize for lying to you in an attempt to protect your feelings. I know I inflicted hurt on you I never wished to do.

The next person I cut off was a guy that Jesus showed me in a dream had more sexual demons then I could count. In the physical dream, he watched another man, his friend, raped me and he did nothing. After waking up from that dream, I told God, you don't have to warn me twice like Cheeky. I am cutting this thang off today!! No amount of cash apps or sweet words could keep me. I guess you can say by cutting him off, I let my personal bank go and a man at one time I wished would get his mess in order so we could be together. The crazy thing is when I deleted him on FB, God moved in that whole conversation, and I was so grateful that I was able to minister to him in the end and that blew my mind.

The next person I cut off; I asked God permission to do it with grace. See, it was starting to get hard for me. I went and purchased some beautiful orange lilies and her favorite turtles. I figured that if you are about to rock someone's world that has been in your life for the last ten years, at least do it with class. Besides, she was one of my FAVORITE'S and a poet too. I was so afraid I would forget to tell her just how much she had impacted my life because I am emotional as hell, and I don't trust my emotions. So I wrote a text telling her just how awesome she was. I didn't want to leave out, not one word. By the time she got to my house, her face was beaming as she read my text. She just kept repeating OMG, Nic! That was her nickname for me.

At this moment, my heart was breaking into a thousand pieces. She had no idea what I was about to say to her next. My family walked in on us in the middle of my goodbye speech. I asked her if we could finish our talk in her car. As I sat in the back of her car, I will never forget that look on her face as the tears began to stream down my face. I was overwhelmed with grief in letting my friend go. I cried so many times that it was pitiful; she even tried to twerk in the middle of Braddock with her fur coat on to cheer me up. She had no idea what I was struggling to get out between deep breaths, stuttering, and tears. I told her the truth because I loved my friend. God was severing our relationship, and she couldn't walk with me anymore. She paused as she took in my words. My eyes searched her face as I looked for some kind of confirmation that I was doing the right thing. Then she asked me for one last hug goodbye. I never cried harder than I ever did that day. Shoot, I am crying now as I write this portion.

She was my rider, my friend, and the aunt of my Godchild. Who would I call now to be goofy with and when I needed a listening ear? I stood in the middle of the street, numb, and hurt. She kept saying, be obedient, Nic, and go back in the house. At that moment, she was more mature of a saint than any Christian I knew.

A week afterward, I continued to comment on her FB page. Eventually, she contacted me and asked me to stop. She said if God told me to let her go, then I needed to be fully obedient. I told her I didn't know how, and I couldn't imagine it would be this dang hard. She always had a way of knowing what to say to me in the midst of my spiritual disobedience. She sent me gospel songs to help and told me not to allow her raggedy self to stand in the way of God's work in my life. Because surely, God had someone awesome that he was going to replace her with. I still don't agree with that because some people are just irreplaceable to me. So I daily I pray for her to be saved and cry out to God in some attempt to get my friend back. Because a part of me feels like if she is saved, then he will allow me to be friends with her again, and although it won't be the same, I just can't imagine her going to hell.

These last three friends include my bestie, my pooh, and my longest childhood friend and the mother of my Godson. I still haven't mustered up the courage to let them go yet.

Every time I muster up the courage to follow through, my heart breaks all over again. I even prayed and asked God to give me a sign they are part of the 8. He confirmed in only ways Jesus can talk to you. Then he told me obedience is better than sacrifice. I will cut off my pooh next, and I know it will be an ugly breakup. We have been rocking for 15+ years, and she is like family to me. If she calls, I always come running even when she doesn't call. She is always trying to fight my battles and beat up anyone that dares to disrespect me. However, a part of me in this last year has grown tired of the friendship. She also has tried to end our friendship in the past three times over the stupidest things. I am convinced if it had not been for my maturity to forgive, we would not have made it this far. After the last time she tried to cut me off, I told myself no more.

I am a bomb friend, and if she views me as being so disposable in her life, then I will allow her to feel my absence. I have gone over a thousand times in my head what to say even though I know no words will be perfect enough. So, I sent these texts pouring out my heart and reassuring her because pooh is hot-headed but that's just how much I love her and how she has impacted my life. My pooh is my family and my sister girl at heart, and I love everything about her crazy self, even though we may disagree at times, God broke the mold when he created her opinionated self.

I love my adopted nephews, her sons. I know my heart will break in a thousand more pieces when I cut her off. I am only prolonging the hurt, and I'm praying to do it with grace. Maybe one last meal as a family so she can talk mess and twerk, and we both jam out to SWV or our favorite Toni Braxton song. Pooh always gives me the big spoon to sing my parts in the song. I will give her flowers while she can still appreciate them because even though the chick ain't dead, a part of me is mourning, and I have to let go.

The last two people are the hardest ones. My bestie, my rider, my google, and Kelly Monique. No words can sum up what she means to me. She too is my sister-friend. My family loves her, which makes this even harder. She has helped me to pick out every apartment I have ever lived in. She is always there when I make big decisions because I trust her judgment. I don't know what her goodbye looks like; I just know that it will rock my world literally.

I mean, who else will come over to my house to raid my fridge and volunteer me to do the cooking. I will miss how we can have the most fun while completely doing nothing at all. Yeah, Kelly is irreplaceable, so I'm praying hard for her, and that God will come back and say something different. I want her to be by my side when this book becomes a bestseller, and we make it to Oprah's couch. She always believes in me when no one else can see the vision. Those types of people are HARD to come by.

However, my yes is for real when it comes to Jesus. God reminded me of a promise I made to him at the altar when I was 7 or 8 years old, and I told the pastor what I wanted from Jesus. Most kids ask for prayers for their moms and dads, but no, I had to be extra. See, I have been extra my whole life. I told the pastor, and I quote, "If no one will go, Lord, send me." I didn't know the magnitude of my words at the time, but when I was complaining one day about all my struggles and asking God why. He reminded me of that moment at the altar. Many are called, but few are chosen. The Bible declares David as a man after God's own heart, not because he was so perfect. In fact, most minsters love to zoom in on his adultery and use it as a point to drive home their sermon. However, Jesus is not like this.

David was a man after his own heart because he had a heart of repentance. No matter how many times he made mistakes and man did he make several. David asks God not to take his spirit away from him. Even after the child produced from adultery dies. He washes his face, puts on his royal clothing, eats, and worships God. Jesus knows no matter what He asks me to do; I will do it, even the hard things that don't display me in the best light. If he asks me to forsake my mother and father, I will do that too. No one means more to me than Jesus, not even Legacy, and I love him more than anything on this earth.

God knows I can't take these people with me, and some have even outstayed their welcome. I don't know what the remainder of 2020 looks like for me. I do know I will cry a lot more tears as I grieve 20 and 15-year friendships. These people were more than friends; they were the family I chose, and I would gladly choose them again. I refuse to change my forward in this book because, at the time, that is how I felt.

When I first started my book, my relationship with my mother didn't exist. I had unforgiveness in my heart towards her and a lot of hurt. Although our relationship may not be perfect, God has done a complete 360 in our lives. I have my mother's back, and I will do everything it takes to hold on and cultivate that relationship. She has to learn me all over again and the same. I thought that the last chapter was truly the last.

However, I woke up this morning feeling in my spirit that God wanted me to write this conclusion as well. I am blessed to have known each one of these wonderful people, and if you have a relationship with them, I will call you blessed too. When my book goes public and it will. I will make sure to give credit to Jesus 1st for the inspiration. I will then acknowledge the dope women that played a part in my village. I couldn't have got here without you. I will continue to do the work because you guys deserve to see the fruits of your labor poured into me down through the years. They say you're a product of the company you keep, well, my little half a circle as I always called it, was spectacular. Your love for me may change after we go our separate ways, but the mind won't.

My best friend doesn't understand how I can still make myself available to those who have hurt me, or those who I have cut off. By definition, she says that is fake, and what would be the point. I told her by the contrary, my ability to love those who have hurt me, is in fact, not fake, but the greatest example of God's grace and love.

See, when I love someone, I love them for life! And although they may no longer have access to my heart and me like they did before, but if they are ever hungry, I will feed them. If they are homeless, if God nudges me to do so, I will provide a place to stay. Lastly, if they are stranded at 2 am in the morning, and they call me, I will still come running. Because that is simply just the way my heart is set up. People don't have to understand, and Kelly and I may not agree on this one. Though if she is ever on her sickbed, you better believe I am showing up to the hospital with a prayer. I just felt the need to say all that. The only way any of those actions will change towards my family is if Jesus forbids me to go or says otherwise. Now, this I promise is the end of my book because I am tired of crying...

Made in the USA
Middletown, DE
10 June 2021